Cambridge E

T0277563

Elements in Politics and Society in Latin America
edited by
Maria Victoria Murillo
Columbia University
Juan Pablo Luna
The Pontifical Catholic University of Chile
Tulia G. Falleti
University of Pennsylvania
Andrew Schrank
Brown University

THE POLITICS OF TRANSITIONAL JUSTICE IN LATIN AMERICA

Power, Norms, and Capacity Building

Ezequiel A. Gonzalez-Ocantos
University of Oxford

CAMBRIDGE
UNIVERSITY PRESS

CAMBRIDGE
UNIVERSITY PRESS

University Printing House, Cambridge CB2 8BS, United Kingdom

One Liberty Plaza, 20th Floor, New York, NY 10006, USA

477 Williamstown Road, Port Melbourne, VIC 3207, Australia

314–321, 3rd Floor, Plot 3, Splendor Forum, Jasola District Centre,
New Delhi – 110025, India

79 Anson Road, #06–04/06, Singapore 079906

Cambridge University Press is part of the University of Cambridge.

It furthers the University's mission by disseminating knowledge in the pursuit of
education, learning, and research at the highest international levels of excellence.

www.cambridge.org
Information on this title: www.cambridge.org/9781108799089
DOI: 10.1017/9781108869973

First published 2020

A catalogue record for this publication is available from the British Library.

ISBN 978-1-108-79908-9 Paperback
ISSN 2515-5245 (print)
ISSN 2515-5253 (online)

The Politics of Transitional Justice in Latin America

Power, Norms, and Capacity Building

Elements in Politics and Society in Latin America

DOI: 10.1017/9781108869973
First published online: January 2020

Ezequiel A. Gonzalez-Ocantos
University of Oxford

Author for correspondence: Ezequiel A. Gonzalez-Ocantos,
ezequiel.gonzalez@nuffield.ox.ac.uk

Abstract: How has Latin America pioneered the field of transitional justice (TJ)? Do approaches vary across the region? This Element describes Latin American innovations in trials and truth commissions, and evaluates two influential models that explain variation in TJ outcomes: the Huntingtonian and Justice Cascade approaches. It argues that scholars should complement these approaches with one that recognizes the importance of state capacity building and institutional change. To translate domestic/international political pressure and human rights norms into outcomes, states must develop 'TJ capabilities'. Not only should states be willing to pursue these highly complex policies, they must also develop competent bureaucracies.

Keywords: Transitional Justice, Latin America, Human Rights, International Law

ISBNs: 9781108799089 (PB), 9781108869973 (OC)
ISSNs: 2515-5245 (print), 2515-5253 (online)

Contents

Introduction

How do nations heal the wounds inflicted by violence? Is it possible to bring solace to victims of egregious human rights violations? Can states fulfil their international obligation to avoid impunity while at the same time cementing democracy and peace? These were some of the questions that Latin American countries faced in the aftermath of the most recent episodes of authoritarian rule and internal armed conflict. As O'Donnell and Schmitter put it in their 1986 classic *Transitions from Authoritarian Rule*:

> We are here in a situation of most difficult ethical, as well as political, choice. Morality is not as fickle and silent as it was when Machiavelli wrote his expediential maxims of political prudence; transitional actors must satisfy not only vital interests but also vital ideals – standards of what is decent and just. Consensus among leaders to bury the past may prove ethically unacceptable to most of the population. All our cases demonstrate the immense difficulty of this dilemma. (1986: 30)

Indeed, processes of democratization and pacification in the 1980s and 1990s were accompanied by intense debates around the issue of transitional justice (TJ), including whether and how to prosecute those responsible for forced disappearances and torture, establish bodies capable of producing authoritative accounts of the causes and consequences of the violence, and recognize and remember victims' suffering.

As O'Donnell and Schmitter also pointed out, mastering the past poses a special kind of dilemma: 'one that simply cannot be avoided and one that the leaders must attempt to resolve' (1986: 75, n. 16). What they perhaps did not anticipate is that far from being circumscribed to transitional moments, this dilemma and the debates it inevitably triggered would become a permanent feature of the political landscape across Latin America, pitting pro- and anti-impunity coalitions in heated conflicts over memory, institutions, and the law. Interestingly, the protracted nature of victims' struggles, and the recurrence of backlash against progress in the direction of truth, justice, and peace, turned the region into a unique site of both innovation in TJ policies and extreme diversity in the shape and success of such policies – a trajectory that continues to the present day. This Element takes stock of these innovations and explores the factors that explain why some societies moved in the direction of accountability for human rights violations whereas others did not. It also reflects upon the reasons that make the Latin American experience such a decisive one in the genealogy of the global TJ paradigm.

What is TJ? According to the United Nations (2004: 4), the term 'comprises the full range of processes and mechanisms associated with a society's attempt to come to terms with a legacy of large-scale past abuses, in order to ensure accountability, serve justice and achieve reconciliation'. Prominent TJ mechanisms include prosecutions and trials against actors thought to be directly or indirectly responsible for the perpetration of crimes during dictatorships and armed conflicts. These proceedings are usually conducted in national courts (Olsen, Payne, and Reiter 2010). Due to the technical and political difficulties that characterize judicialization, national courts are not always capable or willing to process human rights cases. When that happens, trials sometimes take place in international tribunals. For example, in the 1990s the United Nations Security Council created two ad hoc tribunals to deal with specific instances of mass human rights violations: the international criminal tribunals for the former Yugoslavia (1993) and Rwanda (1994). In 2000, the internationalization of accountability mechanisms received a further boost with the creation of a permanent International Criminal Court (Sikkink 2011: 110–121).

TJ mechanisms are not exclusively punitive in nature. Another prominent approach focuses on truth seeking via the creation of commissions charged with investigating patterns of abuse and issuing reports that produce an 'officially proclaimed and publicly exposed truth' (Zalaquett 1995: 6), assess the root causes of the violence, and propose ways to prevent it from recurring (United Nations 2004: 17). TJ processes also focus on repairing the victims, both monetarily and symbolically – for instance, by encouraging states to issue public apologies or build memorial sites (de Greiff 2008). Finally, some TJ mechanisms delve into the terrain of institutional reform, including efforts to vet security and judicial bureaucracies with the aim of expunging those who perpetrated, aided, or abetted serious crimes (Mayer-Reickh and de Grieff 2008). While not always adopted concurrently, trials, truth-seeking initiatives, reparations, and institutional reforms can work in an interdependent manner to compensate for the limitations of each individual mechanism to materialize the rights to truth, justice, and peace. Importantly, the specific features of these mechanisms vary significantly across national contexts. Indeed, the UN emphatically warns against promoting 'one-size-fits-all formulas' and instead encourages a 'thorough analysis of national needs and capacities' before defining the contours of TJ policies (United Nations 2010: 5).

Adopting some form of TJ has gradually become a legal and moral imperative, the 'thing states do' (or at least debate) almost as a matter of course when facing large-scale human rights abuses. This shift in behavioural expectations happened in close connection to changes in the way states understand their obligations vis-à-vis their own citizens and the international community. Such transformations include a growing recognition of the existence of an international 'duty (a) to investigate, prosecute and punish those accused of serious rights violations; (b) to reveal to victims and society at large all known facts and circumstances of past abuses; (c) to provide victims with restitution, compensation and rehabilitation; and (d) to ensure repetition of such violations is prevented' (United Nations 2015: 4–5). The affirmation and substantive content of these duties is the product of the progressive thickening of the corpus of international law via the adoption of instruments such as the International Covenant on Civil and Political Rights (1966), the Convention Against Torture (1984), the Jionet Principles Against Impunity (1997), and the International Convention for the Protection of All Persons from Enforced Disappearance (2006), as well as through the expansive interpretation of these instruments as rendered by bodies such as the Inter-American Court of Human Rights. This legal evolution mainstreamed and normalized TJ to the point that 'the question for the UN', and for most transitioning societies affected by violence, 'is never whether to pursue accountability and justice, but rather when and how' (United Nations 2010: 4).

The way we understand TJ has been fundamentally shaped by historical experience. While the pedigree of some TJ mechanisms dates back to World War II, the paradigm gained notoriety in the 1980s and early 1990s with reference to the policies adopted during regime transitions in South America and Eastern Europe (Orentlicher 1991; Kirtz 1995; Teitel 2000, 2003; Zunino 2019). In fact, definitions of TJ advanced in seminal scholarly works were directly influenced by these experiences. For example, Ruti Teitel (2003: 69, my emphasis), who coined the term in the early 1990s, defines it 'as the conception of justice associated with periods of political change, characterized by legal responses to confront the wrongdoings of repressive *predecessor regimes*'. According to Jon Elster (2004: 1, my emphasis), TJ is 'made up of the processes of trials, purges and reparations that take place after the *transition from one political regime to another*'. Since then, however, the notion of TJ has developed into a powerful legal, political, and discursive apparatus that helps victims in a much wider variety of violence-ridden contexts frame their demands, challenge the acceptability of impunity, and mobilize support. The TJ paradigm has also become a template that influences how international and domestic elites organize institutional responses to these demands under a very diverse set of circumstances. As a field of practice and academic inquiry, TJ is therefore much more encompassing today than it was three decades ago, and this expansion has generated new practical challenges and moral dilemmas.

First, TJ mechanisms are no longer exclusively associated with transitions from authoritarian to democratic regimes, and feature prominently in other kinds of transitions, especially transitions from civil war to peace. In Latin America, for example, TJ was an integral part of peace agreements in

Guatemala (1996), El Salvador (1993), and Colombia (2016). These contexts pose unique challenges for the design, implementation, and success of TJ because armed conflict tends to ravage and severely compromise the institutions responsible for designing and implementing mechanisms such as prosecutions, reparations, and guarantees of non-repetition. By contrast, states emerging from authoritarian rule, where ideas about TJ first developed, usually had more functional institutions, with 'the capacity to make reliable attributions of criminal responsibility, an institutional set-up and the economic capacity to establish large-scale reparations programmes, and institutions sufficiently strong and compliant to withstand reform processes' (United Nations 2017: 8).

Second, TJ is no longer a paradigm or policy tool kit reserved for transitional moments. In fact, human rights prosecutions are still ongoing across Latin America, more than three decades after the onset of the third wave of democratization – a phenomenon that Cath Collins (2011) refers to as 'post-TJ'. Nor are truth commissions strictly reserved for transitional moments, as demonstrated by the cases of Chile, where there have been two commissions since the 1990 transition, and Brazil, where the government established a commission more than twenty years after the transition. More interesting is the use of TJ mechanisms *before* there is any type of transition. For example, following negotiations with paramilitary groups in 2005, several years before the comprehensive ceasefire agreed with FARC rebels in 2016, the Colombian government sponsored a TJ framework known as the Justice and Peace Law. The goal of this initiative was to encourage the demobilization of paramilitary forces and the production of 'truth' in the form of confessions, in exchange for reduced sentences (LaPlante and Theidon 2006). Similarly, victims of the wave of disappearances unleashed by the onset of the 'war on drugs' between Mexican cartels and the military in the mid-2000s quickly adopted the discourse of TJ to frame their demands and promote institutional innovations to help them find their loved ones. Academics, civil society organizations, and even the state also look to the paradigm of TJ in search of possible solutions to this tragedy. As a recent report commissioned by the Mexican National Human Rights Commission puts it, 'the victim count is in the thousands. Ordinary judicial institutions and mechanisms have not been able to address this serious situation and its consequences. The answer many states have found to similar problems is the design and implementation of a TJ policy' (CIDE 2018: 1). In situations such as these, TJ mechanisms initially designed to deal with the causes and consequences of past suffering are pushed into much trickier situations in which violence is still ongoing, perpetrators remain at large, and there is a wider and murkier variety of actors involved, including paramilitaries and drug cartels.

Compounding things further is the fact that these are contexts devoid of the political oxygen generated by moments of clean rupture.

Third, TJ is not associated with strictly punitivist conceptions of justice. This is partly because the theory and practice of TJ gradually elevated the legal and moral standing of alternative goals such as reconciliation. The global reputation of the South African Truth and Reconciliation Commission set up in 1995 played an important part in this process (Rowen 2018). Moreover, the historical record suggests that, for better or for worse, amnesty provisions are very much part of the menu of TJ mechanisms that states consider when seeking to address past violence (Mallinder 2008; Olsen, Payne, and Reiter 2010; Lessa and Payne 2012). This may sound odd given that amnesties are designed to stop or prevent criminal prosecutions against actors responsible for human rights violations – i.e. they stand in the way of 'justice'. But the reality is that in the 1980s and 1990s, debates about the legality and effectiveness of amnesties were central to most TJ processes in Latin America (and elsewhere), either because governments proposed amnesties as a response to instability triggered by prosecutions (Sikkink 2011: 146), or because amnesties formed an integral part of the TJ bargain struck during transitional moments. While a regional and international norm against impunity subsequently gained momentum, contemporary developments – for example, those related to the Colombian peace process – have started to carve out a new discursive and legal space for amnesties in the TJ tool kit. This departure from strictly punitivist conceptions of TJ stems from the realization that when it comes to mastering violent pasts, there are no silver bullets. Reconciling competing objectives such as retribution, truth, and stability can be incredibly difficult. The TJ paradigm is therefore less a ready-made policymaking template and more 'a set of legal, political, and moral dilemmas about how to deal with past violence' (Sharp 2012: 780).

Latin American countries have made crucial contributions to the history, evolution, and meaning of TJ, producing important innovations in the way states respond to victims' demands for truth and justice. In so doing, the Latin American experience has shaped the aspirations of victims and governments worldwide. Section 1 of this Element reviews efforts to advance TJ in Latin America. In what ways have Latin American countries been pioneers in the field of TJ? How has the Latin American experience contributed to the evolution of global TJ norms, redrawing the boundaries of what is imaginable, permissible, and desirable as countries grapple with violent pasts and presents? And how do approaches to TJ vary across the region? The focus will be on describing innovation and variation in the two areas that elicit the most passionate political debates: criminal prosecutions and amnesty laws, as well as truth-telling efforts.

The rest of the Element identifies the political and institutional sources of variation in the success and scope of TJ efforts. I do this in three ways. Section 2, provides a synthesis and evaluation of two influential explanatory approaches: the 'Huntingtonian Model', which emphasizes the centrality of domestic power politics; and the 'Justice Cascade Model', which emphasizes the role of social movements and international norm entrepreneurship. Section 3 makes the case that scholars should complement these dominant approaches with one that recognizes the importance of capacity building and institutional change in TJ processes. The Huntingtonian and Justice Cascade models tend to overlook the difficulties that plague the actual implementation of TJ. In order to translate domestic/international political pressure and human rights norms into concrete outcomes, states must develop what I call 'TJ capabilities'. The capabilities approach highlights the technical dimension of TJ efforts: state actors not only need to be *willing* to pursue these highly complex policies, but must also recruit bureaucratic agents with specific skills and institutional dispositions. Three case studies illustrate the heuristic power of this framework. Section 4 concludes, with a discussion of the historical and structural determinants of Latin America's pivotal role in the history of TJ.

1 Latin American Innovations

In this section I take stock of Latin America's key contributions to the history of TJ, with a focus on criminal prosecutions and amnesty laws, as well as truth commissions. The case studies also reveal wide-ranging variation in the levels of truth and justice achieved by different countries.

1.1 Criminal Prosecutions and Amnesty Laws

Human rights prosecutions are perhaps the most demanding form of TJ. When members of the armed forces or political leaders run the risk of going to jail, the stakes increase dramatically and may lead to instability. Prosecutions and trials also present a number of legal challenges. They involve incredibly complex and unusual investigations, which tend to strain the knowledge and resources of ordinary judicial actors. In particular, judges and prosecutors must balance conflicting legal imperatives emanating from domestic and international sources of law regarding the possibility of prosecuting these crimes. For example, they must answer questions about the legality of amnesties, increasingly repudiated by international law, or the applicability of statutes of limitations for crimes committed in the distant past (Roht-Arriaza 1995, 2015; Gonzalez-Ocantos 2016a: 43–54). In answering these questions, 'the attempt to impose accountability through criminal law often raised rule-of-law dilemmas, including retroactivity in the law, tampering with existing laws, a high degree of prosecutorial selectivity, and a compromised judiciary' (Teitel 2003: 67). The resulting jurisprudence does not always follow 'core principles of legality ... the very essence of the rule of law in ordinary times' (Teitel 2000: 215). In what follows I review how Latin American courts navigated the politically and technically daunting world of criminal prosecutions.

1.1.1 The Argentine Breakthrough of the 1980s

According to Kathryn Sikkink (2008: 2) 'Argentina was the source of an unusually high level of human rights innovation'. Argentina's influence in the development of TJ began in the early 1980s, when the country transitioned to democracy after a military dictatorship (1976–1983). President Alfonsín moved quickly to fulfil his promise to address the tragic legacy of human rights violations. Crucially, the administration introduced a policy of criminal prosecutions that was then without parallel in democracies around the world. The few well-known precedents at the time included the Nuremberg and Tokyo trials, but these had been conducted by international military tribunals, not domestic courts.[1] Alfonsín therefore stepped into unchartered territory. As we shall see, the consequences of his decision to try the military framed formative debates about TJ.

Aware of the dangers of aggravating the military establishment, the president sought to limit the judicialization process to officials with the highest levels of responsibility. He also sponsored legislation that gave military courts original jurisdiction over the proceedings, but time-limited this prerogative to avoid delays or inaction (Osiel 1986; Nino 1996). When the Supreme Council of the Armed Forces proved unwilling to cooperate, the case against the leaders of the military juntas moved to a federal court in the city of Buenos Aires. According to one of the judges:

> People in *Tribunales* [the headquarters of the federal judiciary] did not support us. They were scared, afraid. When we bumped into them in the corridors, they asked us: 'Is it true that you will hold this trial? Are you nuts?' (Gil Lavedra, quoted in Eliaschev 2011; my translation)

Indeed, the trial that ensued was truly unprecedented because for the first time in history a democracy was set to try former military dictators in a civilian court. It was also unprecedented in terms of the sheer complexity of the crimes and the number of hours of witness testimony they would require (Speck 1987). In

---

[1] There was also a less well-known precedent in Greece (Sikkink 2011: 36–50).

December 1985, after months of hard work and intense scrutiny, the judges convicted five junta commanders and acquitted the rest.[2]

The ruling had huge implications for the meaning and future of TJ. First, the court proved that it was possible to assign individual criminal responsibility to those in command of deeply opaque clandestine organizations. Doing so is extremely difficult because such organizations make use of the state apparatus to erase traces of their structures, internal procedures, and activities. Scepticism about the legal viability of prosecutions therefore suffered a blow, and trials were vindicated as a component of what would later become the TJ paradigm. Argentine judges accomplished this feat at a time when the doctrines of international human rights law and criminal law specially designed to facilitate the prosecution and punishment of these crimes were not yet fully in vogue. In fact, international law did not feature prominently in these initial debates about justice in Argentina.[3]

Second, the judges taught the world important lessons about how to prosecute systematic human rights violations. For example, they demonstrated that a selective prosecutorial strategy – i.e. not investigating every single complaint – is often crucial in managing highly complex cases. Furthermore, observers also credit the 1985 trial for introducing and legitimizing distinct evidentiary standards for human rights cases. Argentine judges understood that the types of perpetrators and crimes inevitably force those investigating mass atrocities to rely on indirect and contextual evidence. As a result, courts must be prepared to assign more value to potentially biased or inconsistent witness testimonies than is common in ordinary trials.[4] These witnesses are 'necessary' because they are usually the only available source to reconstruct patterns of clandestine criminal activity and assign individual criminal responsibility. Argentine judges specifically 'noted that the lack of more objective witnesses resulted from the methods of operation chosen by the defendants' (Speck 1987: 506). Enhancing judges' ability to recognize the specificities of human rights crimes, and adapt decision-making templates and standards so that it is possible to succeed in evidence-poor environments, would later become a key focus of those seeking to promote trials elsewhere.

Third, far from putting an end to the trials, the 1985 judgement fuelled further prosecutions. The judges instructed military courts to begin new proceedings

---

[2] Cámara Federal de Apelaciones de la Ciudad de Buenos Aires, *Causa 13/84 Videla, Jorge Rafael y otros*. 9 December 1985.

[3] The ruling relied on criminal definitions included in the criminal code at the time of perpetration rather than on the international criminal categories that would later become a staple in this kind of trial (e.g. crimes against humanity).

[4] For instance, individuals who escaped from clandestine detention centres.

against lower level officers. They did so in open defiance of the Executive's intention to contain the judicialization process. Once again, military judges refused to cooperate, leading federal courts throughout the country to usurp jurisdiction and begin new trials. In December 1986, the government revived its policy of limited prosecutions and imposed a 60-day limit to file new cases (Ley de Punto Final). Judicial personnel responded by extending their working hours, thus allowing victims to file as many cases as possible before the deadline. By February 1987, more than 300 officers were facing judicial proceedings (Acuña and Smulovitz 1995). These developments demonstrated that even if TJ initiatives are carefully orchestrated and centrally planned, they often take on a life of their own – a realization that surely inspired hope among victims, but also fear among elites involved in difficult processes of democratization and pacification. One key lesson in this respect was that the unpredictable nature of TJ is enhanced when such policies are framed in technical terms and conducted within judicial structures governed by relatively autonomous legalistic logics capable of ignoring or defying the limits of political possibility.

Fourth, the 1985 ruling and its immediate consequences led to backlash from the military establishment. Indeed, following two military uprisings (Norden 1996), Congress approved a second amnesty law in June 1987 (Ley de Obediencia Debida). The Supreme Court affirmed the constitutionality of the law, effectively killing all momentum in favour of prosecutions. These developments anticipated what would become one of the distinctive characteristics of Latin American politics during the decades that followed: the fluctuating and non-linear nature of TJ achievements. Argentina thus taught the world that TJ achievements cannot be taken for granted.

1.1.2 Defining the Contours of Amnesty

While the 1985 trial was not thought of at the time as an instance of TJ, subsequent political and academic debates about the merits, limitations, and implications of this unique initiative began to define the field and operationalize the meaning of the term.[5] Argentine federal judges had shown that despite being politically and technically challenging, human rights trials were indeed possible. The backlash that ensued – in the form of two amnesty laws and a set of presidential pardons issued in 1990 in favour of the junta commanders – also showed the precarity of criminal accountability during transitional moments.

---

[5] See Arthur (2009: 48–57) for an account of a conference organized in 1988, which played a pivotal role in framing ideas about TJ. The conference was organized partly in response to events taking place in Argentina. See Section 2.

And this contrast spurred seminal discussions about the difficult balance between justice and political stability in TJ processes (see Section 2).

In the realm of politics, however, stability concerns quickly gained the upper hand. Indeed, by the mid-1990s Latin America was drowning in a sea of amnesty laws designed to prevent prosecutions. In Chile (1978) and Brazil (1979), military dictators passed amnesty laws long before regime change was even on the horizon. The Argentine saga of the late 1980s did little to encourage incoming democratic administrations in either country to challenge these provisions. Sikkink (2011: 90) suggests that Chilean elites 'explicitly designed their justice strategy to avoid what they considered the "mistakes" of the Argentine experience'. Similarly, when Uruguayan civil society forced a referendum on the amnesty law passed in 1986 following the 1985 transition, voters decided to play it safe and keep it (Lessa 2012). The agreements that put an end to Central American civil wars also led to the adoption of amnesty laws in El Salvador (1993) and Guatemala (1996). And when the violence of Peru's internal armed conflict subsided, President Fujimori passed an amnesty law in 1995 that shielded civilian and military officials involved in counterterrorism operations from the threat of criminal prosecutions.

All of these laws severely constrained the possibility of implementing TJ. For example, by the mid-1990s several Supreme Courts – including those of Argentina, Chile, El Salvador, and Peru – had declared the constitutionality of the amnesties. Such decisions are a testament to the weakness of the international anti-impunity norm at the time. Judges and politicians did not yet feel bound by the international legal doctrines that in subsequent years would lead to a more or less generalized repudiation of amnesties. Some courts did not believe international law was directly applicable, especially if the relevant treaties had come into effect after the perpetration of the crimes. For others, the legality of amnesties was a strictly political question, and one that the courts should not try to answer. Yet other judges looked to certain international instruments, most notably Protocol II of the 1949 Geneva Conventions, to show the lack of an international consensus on the need to repeal amnesty laws (Roht-Arriaza and Gibson 1998).[6]

In sum, courts found a variety of reasons to legitimize amnesties and thus block prosecutions. The impunity regimes constructed on the back of these interpretations proved extremely resilient. Argentina's laws of Punto Final and Obediencia Debida stayed on the books until 2005. In Uruguay and El Salvador, the amnesties were only declared unconstitutional in 2009 and 2016, respectively. Peru's was the shortest-lived amnesty: it was only in force between 1995

---

[6] Protocol II allows amnesties after the end of 'hostilities'.

and 2001. It was nevertheless an obstacle for prosecutions for several years after that. At the time of writing, amnesty laws are still on the books in Brazil, Chile, and Guatemala.[7]

Latin American amnesty laws were significant not only because they narrowed down the space for prosecutions, but also because they helped define stricter standards regarding what is acceptable when it comes to impunity and fuelled unparalleled creativity among human rights activists across the region. To understand this seeming paradox, it helps to explore important differences between the aforementioned amnesty provisions.

Amnesties such as those passed in Brazil, Chile, Uruguay, El Salvador, and Peru are often described as 'blanket' amnesties, meaning that they barred prosecutions for any crime perpetrated in the context of state-sponsored terrorism or counter-insurgency operations. By contrast, other amnesties, including Argentina's Ley de Obediencia Debida and Guatemala's Ley de Reconciliación Nacional, introduced highly consequential exceptions. In 1983, President Alfonsín sent to Congress a bill to nullify the self-amnesty law approved by the military before the transition. The government sought to include in the law a clause that would exempt those who had followed orders from any criminal responsibility, but groups in Congress sponsored amendments that expanded the universe of cases susceptible to prosecution. When the law was passed, it stated that officers who had followed orders would be exempt from any criminal responsibility *except* when they had perpetrated 'atrocious and abhorrent' acts. This constituted the basis for the avalanche of investigations launched after the 1985 trial. Several years later, the Ley de Obediencia Debida did not mention 'atrocious or abhorrent' acts, possibly in an attempt to avoid interpretations that could risk another wave of indictments, but nevertheless introduced notable exceptions, including the kidnapping of minors. Guatemala's 1996 amnesty law was much more specific in terms of exclusions. Article 8 mandates that the amnesty shall not apply to the crimes of genocide, torture, or forced disappearance, or those for which there is no statute of limitations or for which amnesty is prohibited under Guatemalan or international law. Until recently, this was the only amnesty provision in the Americas that made explicit reference to international crimes.

These laws represent milestones in the history of TJ in Latin America for at least two reasons. First, even in these early stages, and despite the political duress these countries were under, it was clear that political expediency and amnesty proposals already found limits in the type of impunity society could

---

[7] As we shall see, courts in Chile and Guatemala interpret the applicability of amnesty provisions in ways that enable varying degrees of criminal accountability.

tolerate. For instance, the exclusion of kidnapping of minors from the 1987 Ley de Obediencia Debida was an obvious consequence of the deep support for the struggle of the Grandmothers of Plaza de Mayo, who continued to denounce the disappearance not only of their children, but also of their grandchildren, many of them born in clandestine detention centres. In this sense, the exceptions in the Argentine and Guatemalan amnesties track the emergence of a regional anti-impunity norm that questions the validity of blanket amnesties. Importantly, these exceptions themselves reinforced the cycle of international norm development, contributing to the consolidation of a legal vocabulary that was later used to challenge or limit amnesty provisions. The 1996 Guatemalan peace accords illustrate how this worked in practice. The UN took advantage of its role as facilitator of the negotiations in order to experiment with the operationalization of clearer criteria regarding the validity of amnesties. Today, UN guidelines encourage officials to 'reject any endorsement of amnesty for genocide, war crimes, or crimes against humanity, including those relating to ethnic, gender and sexually based international crimes [and] ensure that no such amnesty previously granted is a bar to prosecution before any United Nations-created or assisted court' (United Nations 2004: 21). But as Douglas Cassel explains, in 1996 'UN officials simply did not know which crimes could be amnestied without transgressing the murky boundaries of relevant human rights and humanitarian law' (Cassel 1996: 222). The Guatemalan experience contributed to the specification of those boundaries.

Second, these exceptions created cracks in impunity regimes. Activists and their lawyers would skilfully exploit such cracks in their relentless pursuit of justice. As we shall see, court cases involving the kidnapping of minors became the Achilles' heel of Argentina's impunity laws in the late 1990s, unleashing a wave of trials without precedent in the world. Similarly, exceptions included in Guatemala's amnesty law triggered incessant battles over the meaning of those exceptions, keeping the promise of criminal accountability alive in the courts and gradually widening windows of opportunity for more ambitious accountability efforts (Braid and Roht-Arriaza 2012). Overall, these and other amnesties became an engine of innovation in TJ because they forced victims and their lawyers to be creative whenever they brought arguments to court. Such efforts spurred regional debates that influenced the development of standards that domestic and international courts now use to assess the legality of blanket amnesties, and, where blanket amnesties remain on the books, the criteria applied to limit their reach. All of this fuelled an exceptionally productive journey that culminated in key regional and global landmarks in the history of human rights trials. In what follows, I take stock of those achievements.

1.1.3 Waves and Landmarks

By the mid-1990s it was clear that the question of criminal prosecutions would not go away. In fact, human rights lawyers and judges started to develop a series of important juridical innovations that led to unprecedented trial waves in Argentina and Chile, and human rights trials of global significance elsewhere. Table 1 summarizes the outcome of accountability efforts in nine countries.

Argentina stands out because of the scope and effectiveness of trials since the 1980s. It took only a few years after the approval of the amnesties for courts to reactivate cases. They did so in a very unusual way. Instead of launching ordinary criminal investigations with punitive intent, judges first carried out 'truth trials'.[8] In a series of briefs filed before a federal appeals court in the city of Buenos Aires in 1995, human rights victims argued that despite the limits on criminal prosecutions imposed by the amnesty provisions, the judiciary could still investigate the fate of the disappeared. In other words, courts could expand their remit to act as fact-finding bodies without necessarily assigning individual criminal responsibility. This gradually led judges to recognize that under international law, victims and their families had a 'right to truth'. Initially, courts showed reluctance to go beyond sending formal information requests to the executive branch and the armed forces. Quite predictably, these requests produced no breakthroughs.[9] By 1997, however, several judges had developed a more robust understanding of the implications of an internationally recognized right to truth, and were prepared to make bolder moves. For instance, they admitted new witness testimonies and deposed military officers, in some cases ordering the arrest of those who refused to cooperate. As the 'truth trials' gained momentum, hearings became part of the daily routine of many federal courts, exposing old and new judges to a wealth of evidence. This experience further invested a critical mass of judicial actors in the human rights cause. In their eyes, the amnesty laws blocked action in cases where there was now clear evidence warranting further measures – a situation they were not willing to tolerate for much longer.

Human rights lawyers also exploited loopholes in the amnesty provisions. According to the Grandmothers of Plaza de Mayo, the military dictatorship was responsible for the kidnapping of at least 500 hundred babies. These crimes were not included in the 1987 Ley de Obediencia Debida. Beginning in 1996, their lawyers bombarded federal judges with cases that showed the systematic

---

[8] For a detailed account of the truth trials see Roth-Arriaza (2006: 101–108) and Gonzalez-Ocantos (2016a: 96–105).

[9] One of the original cases eventually made it to the Inter-American Commission, ending in a friendly settlement with the government in 1999.

Table 1 Outcome of criminal accountability efforts in nine Latin American countries

Country	Amnesty	Trials
Argentina		
Transition: 1983 Violence: Approx. 9,000 disappeared (CONADEP 1984); victim associations estimate 30,000 disappearances.	Ley de Punto Final (1986) Ley de Obediencia Debida (1987) Presidential pardons (1990) The Supreme Court declared the amnesties and pardons unconstitutional in 2005 and 2010, respectively.	3,081 individuals have faced charges (December 2018) 221 completed trials (December 2018) 915 convictions; 144 acquittals (July 2019) Sources: www.cels.org.ar/ web/estadisticas-delitos-de-lesa-humanidad/; www.fis cales.gob.ar/lesa-humani dad/juicios-en-numeros -durante-2018-finalizaron- 17-debates-y-aumento-la-cantidad-de-imputados-con-prision-domiciliaria/
Brazil		
Transition: 1985 Violence: Approx. 400 dead/disappeared (Abrão and Torelly 2012)	Ley No. 6,683/1979 (1979) Still on the books	Starting in 2008, prosecutors launched 36 criminal cases. All but two dismissed by the courts. No convictions Source: Lessa (2019)
Chile		
Transition: 1990 Violence: 3,197 dead/ disappeared (Collins 2011); approx. 28,000 torture survivors according to the 2004 Valech Report	Decreto Ley 2,191 (1978) Still on the books, but in 1998 the Supreme Court ruled that it cannot prevent investigations	332 completed criminal cases (June 2018) 251 final Supreme Court rulings between June 2010 – June 2018 788 convictions; 118 acquittals (June 2018) Source: Collins (2018)
El Salvador		
Peace Accords: 1992 Violence: 75,000 dead/disappeared	Ley de Amnistía General para la	Until mid-2015: at least 68 cases filed; 34 in pre-trial stage; 26 shelved; 2

Table 1 (cont.)

Country	Amnesty	Trials
(Betancour, Figuereido, and Buergenthal 1993)	Consolidación de la Paz (1993) The Supreme Court declared the amnesty law unconstitutional in 2016.	acquittals and 6 convictions Source: Martínez-Barahona and Gutiérrez-Salazar (2016)
Guatemala Peace Accords: 1996 Violence: 200,000 dead/disappeared (Brett 2016)	Ley de Reconciliación Nacional (1996) Still on the books, but in 2008 the Constitutional Court ruled that the law could not be applied to serious human rights violations	Since 2009: 30+ military officers/paramilitaries and one rebel have been convicted, and 21+ await trial 2013: Former dictator Ríos-Montt convicted. Constitutional court annulled the conviction and ordered a retrial. Source: Burt (2016)
Mexico Transition: 2000 Violence: In 2001 the National Human Rights Commission documented 275 disappearance cases during the 1970s' 'dirty war'. Estimates by victim groups vary widely but are usually higher (Gonzalez-Ocantos 2016a: 208–213)	No amnesty	Special prosecutor appointed in 2001 filed around 15 cases of violations perpetrated during the 1960 and 1970s. The Special Prosecutor's Office was dismantled in 2006 with no convictions. In 2009 one case ended with a 5-year conviction against a former intelligence agent. Sources: Gonzalez-Ocantos (2016a); Yankelevich (2018)
Paraguay Transition: 1989	No amnesty	9 prosecutions and 8 convictions between 1999 and 2008

Table 1 (cont.)

Country	Amnesty	Trials
Violence: According to 2009 truth commission report, 396 disappeared and 2,691 torture victims		Source: Lessa (2019)
Peru		
Transition: 2000 Violence: Approx. 70,000 dead/disappeared (Comisión de la Verdad y Reconciliación 2003)	Ley de Amnistía (1995) Challenged by a lower court in 1995 but reinstated immediately Transitional government complied with a 2001 Inter-American ruling that invalidated the law. Subsequently, the Constitutional Court affirmed the unconstitutionality of the law.	700+ military officers investigated since 2001 44+ trials at the Sala Penal Nacional since 2006 71 convictions; 118 acquittals; several re-trials 2008–2010: trials against *Grupo Colina* in Special Anti-Corruption Court); 25 convictions; 16 acquittals 2009: Conviction against former President Fujimori. Source: Gonzalez-Ocantos (2016a)
Uruguay		
Transition: 1985 Violence: According to an official report released in 1985, 184 executions and forced disappearances during the 1973–1984 dictatorship. Victims estimate that the number of political prisoners and torture victims is much higher (Lessa 2012)	Ley de Caducidad de las Pretenciones Punitivas del Estado (1986) The Supreme Court declared the amnesty law unconstitutional in 2009	302 cases filed since 1980s 94 shelved 13 final rulings 20 convictions Source: www .observatorioluzibarburu. org/reportes/

nature of the plan to abduct babies born in clandestine detention centres and give them up for adoption. This eventually convinced at least three judges to place high-ranking military officers in pre-trial detention. Some of these decisions were heavily grounded in international human rights law, and, for the first time, characterized the special status of forced disappearances and torture as 'crimes against humanity'. Crucially, in one of the cases, lawyers were able to show that the kidnappers had also participated in the disappearance of the child's parents. This presented the court with an uncomfortable contradiction: it could indict the defendants for abducting a baby, but not for disappearing her parents – arguably a more serious crime. Skilful coordination between human rights lawyers and the judge led to a historic ruling in 2001 that resolved this contradiction: it declared the unconstitutionality of the amnesties.[10] The judge defined the crime of forced disappearance as a crime against humanity, and therefore one that cannot be amnestied under international law. The ruling was a remarkable achievement because at this stage the Inter-American Court of Human Rights had yet to produce an opinion on the legality of amnesties (see Section 2).[11]

These developments diffused acceptance of an innovative legal vocabulary firmly anchored in international human rights law, clearing a path towards accountability. Defining the debate in technical terms and linking justice to the state's international obligations also insulated the process from political pressure at a time when successive presidential administrations opposed prosecutions. While the 2001 ruling did not remove the amnesty, it did provide justification for other lower courts to refuse to automatically dismiss cases. Instead, judges started to argue that the applicability of the amnesty should be evaluated case by case, and that the law did not preclude the possibility of investigating serious allegations. On the basis of this arduous process of legal innovation, Argentine courts unleashed an unprecedented programme of criminal prosecutions. A change in the political orientation of the executive following the election of President Kirchner in 2003 added momentum to the process. Kirchner made criminal prosecutions a centrepiece of his programme, and promoted new judges to the Supreme Court. In 2005, a much more progressive Supreme Court put an end to the debate about the status of the amnesties in a landmark ruling.[12] In 2010 it also nullified the pardons granted to the junta commanders two decades earlier.[13]

---

[10] Juzgado Nacional en lo Criminal y Correccional No. 4 de la Capital Federal, S*imón, Julio, Del Cerro, Juan s/sustracción de menores de 10 años.* 6 March 2001.

[11] For a detailed account of the kidnapping cases, see Gonzalez-Ocantos (2016a: 105–112).

[12] Corte Suprema de Justicia de la Nación, *Simón, Julio y otros s/privación ilegítima de la libertad.* 14 June 2005.

[13] Corte Suprema de Justicia de la Nación, *Videla, Jorge s/recurso extraordinario.* 26 April 2010.

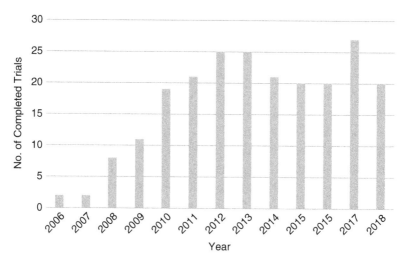

Figure 1 No. of completed trials – Federal Oral Tribunals (2006–2018).
Source: Author, based on Procuraduría de Crímenes Contra la Humanidad (2018)

Starting in 2006, and thanks in part to the testimonies and documents gathered during the trials of the 1990s, Argentina experienced an incredibly quick explosion of human rights prosecutions, the like of which had not been seen before (or, indeed, since) anywhere else in the world. According to official statistics, by December 2018, 3,081 individuals linked to the dictatorship's repressive plan had been asked to appear in court (Procuraduría de Crímenes Contra la Humanidad 2018). By the same date, Federal Oral Tribunals had completed 221 trials (Figure 1). More recent statistics indicate that by July 2019 courts had issued 915 convictions and 144 acquittals (Figure 2). This amounts to an impressive conviction rate of 86.4 per cent. Judges consistently rely on international law to define crimes as crimes against humanity, ignore statutes of limitations, and apply special protocols that facilitate investigative efforts and the assignment of individual criminal responsibility to perpetrators with varying degrees of involvement in the crimes. Importantly, the judicialization process targets not only military officers, but also civilians who played a key role in facilitating state terrorism, including 77 members of the judiciary, 81 intelligence agents, 40 healthcare professionals, 9 priests, and 28 businessmen.[14] As we shall see in Section 3, the Argentine trial wave is responsible for innumerable innovations, ranging from the development of practical guidelines that make it logistically possible to prosecute and punish such a large number of defendants, to the use of

---

[14] See www.cels.org.ar/web/estadisticas-delitos-de-lesa-humanidad/ [accessed, 5 April 2019].

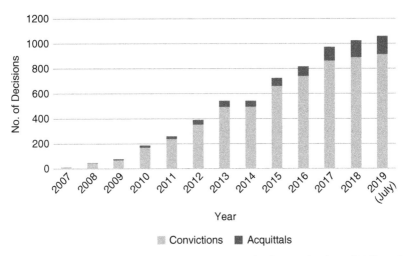

Figure 2 Cumulative no. of convictions and acquittals – Federal Oral Tribunals (2007–2019).

Source: Author, based on CELS, www.cels.org.ar/web/estadisticas-delitos-de-lesa-humanidad/ [accessed 5 April 2019]; and for 2018 and 2019, Procuración General de la Nación, www.fiscales.gob.ar/lesa-humanidad/?tipo-entrada=estadisticas [accessed 4 August 2019]

special evidentiary and jurisprudential techniques designed for the treatment of sexual crimes during state-sponsored terrorism.

Chile has also experienced a trial wave, although there are important contrasts with Argentina. This is a testament to the enormous variation in TJ outcomes that still characterizes Latin America. The democratic regime that emerged in Chile after the 1990 transition was heavily constrained by the lingering power of General Pinochet. This meant that the incoming administration could not entertain the possibility of emulating Alfonsín's policies. Most cases involving human rights violations were either captured by military courts or dismissed by civilian courts invoking the amnesty. Only specific crimes not covered by the amnesty (e.g. the murder of Orlando Letelier in Washington DC, excluded due to pressure from the US government) and crimes perpetrated outside the period from September 1973 to March 1978 initially made it through the courts.[15] These exceptions, however, did not have the same corrosive effects on the amnesty as those exploited by Argentine litigants in the late 1990s. In a report published in 1996, a leading human rights organization concluded that the vast majority of judges still favoured the enforcement of the amnesty 'as

---

[15] Manuel Contreras, head of Pinochet's infamous intelligence agency, and his deputy were convicted in 1993.

a formula to solve human rights cases' (Arzobispado de Santiago 1996: np; my translation).

In 1998, Pinochet's tenure as commander-in-chief of the armed forces came to an end, and the tide began to turn. First, at the start of this crucial year victims filed the first complaints against Pinochet for a series of crimes perpetrated during the so-called caravan of death of 1973 (Roht-Arriaza 2006: 74–79). Juan Guzmán, a Santiago Appeals Court judge, landed the case and proceeded to conduct an extremely meticulous investigation targeting Pinochet and other defendants.[16] Second, the Supreme Court, hitherto controlled by judges appointed by Pinochet, experienced a dramatic change in personnel. The most important immediate consequence of the appointment of several pro-accountability judges was a September ruling maintaining that kidnapping cases in which the body had never been recovered involved ongoing crimes and therefore fell outside the period stipulated in the amnesty law.[17] This was the first major strike against impunity, and it cleared the way for the punishment of hundreds of violations. It also began to crystallize the principle that the amnesty did not block investigations. In other words, before invoking the amnesty, judges first had to establish a series of facts in order to decide whether or not the provision applied to the case in question. Third, Pinochet was arrested in London following an extradition request filed by a Spanish judge investigating crimes perpetrated during the Cóndor Operation. This triggered a diplomatic controversy involving Spanish, British, and Chilean authorities, and prompted the Chilean courts to take human rights cases more seriously (Roht-Arriaza 2006, chapters 1–2).

Over the course of the next several years, accountability efforts gained momentum. In 1999 the Supreme Court upheld Judge Guzmán's decision to disapply the amnesty in the 'caravan of death' case (Collins 2011: 84). Furthermore, when Pinochet returned to Chile in March 2000, the number of complaints filed against him grew exponentially. This led to the first formal charge in January 2001 ('caravan of death' case), and another one in 2004 (Operation Cóndor case). Crucially, between 2001 and 2002 the Supreme Court and the Santiago Court of Appeals appointed special judges to oversee hundreds of human rights cases still making their way through the judiciary, and set up a system to closely supervise their work (Collins and Hau 2016: 137). These judges 'began criss-crossing the country, digging up more mass graves, and calling former military and police officers in for questioning' (Roth-Arriaza 2006: 93). Such efforts paid off. For example, in 2002 a judge convicted a series

---

[16] Cámara de Apelaciones de Santiago, *Rol 2182–98*.
[17] Suprema Corte de Justicia, *Rol 469–98*.

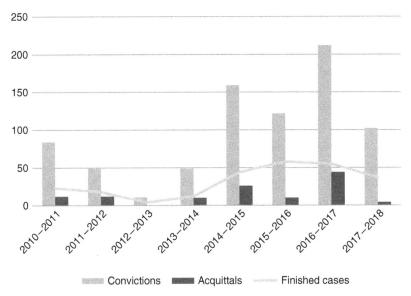

Figure 3 Completed cases, convictions and acquittals – Supreme Court (June 2010 – July 2018).

Source: Author, based on Collins (2018). Each period covers the months from June one year to July the following year.

of defendants in a case involving the murder of a trade union leader, and 'by late September 2004 approximately 300 victims of disappearance and 450 of political execution had cases in the courts' (Collins 2011: 138). As Figure 3 shows, accountability efforts did not stop there, and they continue to the present day. Pinochet himself was never convicted (he died in 2006), but judges have charged hundreds of defendants, mainly in kidnapping and homicide cases. Between June 2010 and July 2018, the Supreme Court issued final decisions in 251 cases, including 788 convictions and 118 acquittals. This amounts to a conviction rate of 87 per cent – almost identical to Argentina's. Many more cases are slowly making their way to the top.

Despite the impressive scope and effectiveness of criminal accountability efforts, the Chilean wave is more limited than the Argentine one. First and foremost, the amnesty law is still on the books. In the early 2000s, courts started to more or less consistently follow the 1998 Supreme Court ruling that disapplied the amnesty in kidnapping cases, but still enforced it in homicide or torture cases. In 2004, the Supreme Court consolidated this restrictive approach when, in a reaction against isolated rulings in which lower courts departed from the general trend, it stated that if the remains of a disappeared person were finally located, the crime should be considered a homicide covered by the amnesty. Some courts subsequently 'allowed uncorroborated testimony to convert the crimes into amnestiable homicide' (Collins 2011: 122), leading to a resurgence of inconsistent treatments of the amnesty across the judiciary. Second, the legal debate gradually expanded to encompass discussion about whether or not the crimes could be categorized as crimes against humanity, and therefore not covered by the amnesty regardless of when they were perpetrated. As a result, the late 2000s saw international law become more central to the judicialization process. But unlike in Argentina, no consensus was ever reached regarding the international nature of dictatorship-era crimes. As Collins (2011: 126) explains in her splendid analysis of the Chilean trial wave, 'the point of contention simply shifted to whether a particular set of acts actually qualified as a war crime or crime against humanity'. This means that plaintiffs are usually at the mercy of the preferences of the judges assigned to their case. It also means that torture cases that do not also involve murder or kidnapping struggle to move forwards or deliver convictions because this particular crime almost always falls within the remit of the amnesty law if not defined as a crime against humanity. Third, since 2008 sentencing criteria has become more lenient, leading to a form of punishment that does live up to the severity of the crimes. Judges suddenly decided to adopt a sui generis formula called 'media prescripción'. This allowed 'sentences to be reduced significantly in cases where over half the allotted statute of limitations period for the crime had elapsed' (Collins and Hau 2016: 140). The Supreme Court thus found a way to circumvent limits on the enforcement of statutes of limitations mandated by international law in cases of crimes against humanity and other serious violations of human rights.

The trial waves in Argentina and Chile are indeed exceptional in terms of scope, effectiveness, and durability.[18] But courts in countries outside the Southern Cone have also left a distinguished mark on the global history of TJ. If Argentina showed the world that criminal prosecutions were possible by holding the first ever human rights trial against former authoritarian leaders in civilian courts, in 2009 Peru demonstrated that domestic courts could similarly convict a democratically elected head of state for masterminding crimes against humanity. And four years later, Guatemalan courts handed down the first ever domestic conviction for genocide against a former head of state in a fair trial.

The armed conflict between the Peruvian state and the Shining Path left an estimated toll of 70,000 deaths between 1980 and 2000. The crimes perpetrated during the conflict include torture, extrajudicial executions, massacres, and

---

[18] See Section 3 for further discussion of differences between the Argentine and Chilean trial waves.

forced disappearances. Hostilities mostly took place under a series of democratically elected administrations. In 1992, President Alberto Fujimori launched a 'self-coup' inaugurating an electoral authoritarian period that lasted until 2000, when his government imploded and he fled to Japan. In subsequent years, Peruvian courts made tremendous progress in terms of criminal accountability. Judges of the Sala Penal Nacional, a high criminal court, presided over more than 44 trials, handing down at least 71 convictions and 118 acquittals. Other lower courts also tried the leaders of the Grupo Colina, a clandestine military-intelligence unit created by Fujimori (Burt 2009: 387), issuing 25 convictions and 16 acquittals (Gonzalez-Ocantos 2016a, chapter 4). While these figures are not as impressive as those of Argentina or Chile, they are by no means insignificant: judges and prosecutors have investigated key massacres perpetrated during all stages of the conflict, developed robust jurisprudential standards heavily anchored in international human rights law, and managed to convict high-profile perpetrators on all sides.

The crown jewel of these achievements is the conviction of former President Fujimori. Hoping to orchestrate a political comeback, Fujimori left Japan in 2005 and travelled to Chile. Peruvian victims and authorities moved quickly to file an extradition request, which was eventually granted in 2007. In itself, this was an important precedent that signalled the absence of safe havens for human rights criminals in Latin America. In line with Peru's constitution, the Supreme Court assigned three justices to a special chamber that would try the former president for the crimes listed in the extradition order. Importantly, they split the docket into three trials, and gave priority to human rights cases. These included the assassination of 15 people in 1991 (*Barrios Altos*), the murder of 10 students and a professor in 1992 (*La Cantuta*), and 2 kidnappings (Burt 2009). The trial involved 161 public sessions, and ended in April 2009 with a ruling that found Fujimori guilty of multiple aggravated counts of homicide, assault, and kidnapping, and sentenced him to 25 years in prison. Crucially, the court concluded that *Barrios Altos* and *La Cantuta* 'are also crimes against humanity, fundamentally, because they were committed within the framework of a state policy of selective but systematic elimination of alleged members of subversive groups' (Supreme Court of Justice of Peru 2010: 802).

The decision was 'pathbreaking' (Méndez 2010: 650) for at least three reasons. First, the court demonstrated the viability of trying a still popular and relatively influential former head of state in a complicated political context. At the time of the trial, Fujimorismo was on track to regain national political significance, and Alan García, the sitting president, not only strongly opposed prosecutions, but also relied on Fujimorista members of Congress to pass legislation (Gonzalez-Ocantos 2016a: 160–162). In this sense, the trial was an example of how TJ mechanisms can become decoupled from broader political dynamics and thus acquire high levels of autonomy. Second, scholars have criticized human rights trials for being wasteful, polarizing, and running the risk of becoming 'show trials'. Writing in the 1990s, Zalaquett (1995: 7) warned that satisfying 'the need to know the full truth while observing the norms for a fair trial has proven very difficult in practice'.the Fujimori trial is proof that domestic courts can effectively navigate these tensions, strictly enforcing the rule of law while at the same time 'delivering a coherent moral message' (Prusak 2010: 871). For example, in addition to affording Fujimori ample opportunities to defend himself, judges were mindful of his health problems, and planned hearings accordingly. There is evidence that this behaviour boosted general trust in judicial institutions (Gonzalez-Ocantos 2016b). Finally, the court was able to establish individual responsibility for crimes the defendant did not directly perpetrate. To do this, the prosecution and the judges opted for a theory of criminal responsibility known as 'mediate authorship' (*autoría mediata*), which implies the existence of an illegal, hierarchically structured organization in which the fungibility of immediate perpetrators guarantees the man behind the scene, i.e. the leader, control over the execution of the plan (Ambos 2011). Mediate authorship is much more demanding than other theories commonly used in international trials against former heads of state, such as 'command responsibility'. Rather than signalling active participation in the crimes, the latter is a crime of omission in which the leader fails to control his subordinates, and therefore is easier to prove. By taking an alternative route, the Peruvian court dramatically increased its burden of proof. The decision, which was confirmed by another panel of Supreme Court judges, thus makes a critical contribution to the growing corpus of law dealing with international and other complex criminal ventures.[19]

Four years later, Latin America landed another 'first' in the history of criminal prosecutions, this time in Guatemala. In 2013, former head of state General Ríos-Montt was convicted of genocide and crimes against humanity, and sentenced to 80 years in prison. The trial, which lasted 53 days, is the most significant of a series of trials against members of the armed forces that started in 2008, and has so far led to the conviction of around 30 low- and mid-ranking officials (Burt 2016).

The conviction for genocide is particularly significant. First, during the Guatemalan peace process there was never any official recognition that geno-cide had taken place, so the ruling vindicated the view that at least during the

---

[19] In developing its own interpretation of mediate authorship, the Supreme Court relied on the 1985 Argentine ruling, which took a similar approach.

1982–1983 period, when the former general was head of state, the government implemented a 'scorched earth' policy designed to destroy indigenous communities. Second, genocide is a notoriously demanding criminal definition. Proving the various constitutive acts of genocide and the intent to destroy a national, ethnic, racial, or religious group is very hard. In fact, prosecutors in other countries usually shy away from filing genocide charges or deal with the crime in woefully inadequate ways. The court's ability to weave a convincing narrative of individual responsibility is therefore impressive and an example for others to follow. The judges relied on the testimonies of 97 witnesses, 39 forensic experts, and 16 expert witnesses, including historians, psychologists, and international lawyers, and innovated in the treatment of this evidence (Brett 2016). For example, in order to prove one of the constitutive acts of genocide – serious bodily or mental harm – the court made a broad interpretation of mental harm. It concluded that the military had used detention camps to 'break the will' of the Maya Ixil population and thus destroy their integrity as a distinct cultural group (Kemp 2014: 139). This form of psychological warfare was key to establishing another of the constitutive acts of genocide: creating conditions that bring about the physical destruction of a group. For the court, cultural destruction entailed an attempt at physical destruction. The judges also relied on military manuals, comparative statistical analysis of deaths in armed conflicts and casualty patterns throughout the country, and expert interpretations of Guatemalan military history to prove the intent to destroy the group, as well as Ríos-Montt's 'essential contribution' to the criminal enterprise (Kemp 2014). In other words, his was not just a crime of omission.

While the trial waves experienced by Argentina and Chile since the early 2000s follow a more or less linear trajectory, the convictions of Fujimori and Ríos-Montt led to backlash, illustrating once again the dynamism of TJ. In Fujimori's case, his family and party relentlessly requested a pardon from at least two presidents, and finally got their way in December 2017, eight years after the conviction. The victims fought back, and got the pardons overturned by international and domestic courts. In Ríos-Montt's case, the backlash was immediate. Ten days after his conviction, a 3–2 decision by the Constitutional Court agreed that his due process rights had been violated and ordered retrial. The former general died before this could ever happen. Guatemalan experts argue that the conviction for genocide made the backlash especially strong, and speculate that, had the court focused on other charges, the story would have been different. The sitting president at the time, a former general who was mentioned by one of the witnesses as an active participant in the repressive campaign of the early 1980s, refused to accept that Guatemala had experienced genocide. Similarly, the business community was appalled by this characterization of the conflict. It feared, on the one hand, irreparable damage to the country's international reputation, and, on the other, calls for progressive economic change to address the structural roots of the crime (Brett 2016; Burt 2016). Attempts to bury the past continue at the time of writing: the Guatemalan Congress is determined to pass a new amnesty law, this time including genocide and crimes against humanity (see Section 3).

The success of criminal prosecutions in many Latin American countries points to the viability of this form of TJ amidst numerous political and technical challenges, and offers a roadmap for other countries still struggling to find a way to fulfil the promise of justice and legal equality. However, such progress should not obscure the fact that impunity always remains a possibility, and is still the norm in some places. In other words, Latin America continues to experience enormous variation in the success of TJ. It is therefore appropriate to end this *tour d'horizon* of criminal prosecutions with two cases that are particularly notable for their lack of progress. In general, cases with a poor record of criminal account-ability are characterized by weaker human rights movements that are unable to manufacture a political consensus around TJ, or transform judicial institutions so as to guarantee receptivity to an unorthodox legal vocabulary anchored in inter-national human rights law (Gonzalez-Ocantos 2016a).

One notable case is Brazil, where the 1979 amnesty law remains on the books and has been upheld by the Supreme Court as recently as 2010. After more than two decades of inactivity following the 1985 transition, the ascendance of the leftist Workers' Party to power in 2002 gradually created more favourable conditions for TJ. In 2008, the chief prosecutor created a special division to investigate dictatorship-era crimes. This resulted in around 300 investigations, of which only a limited number reached the courts. Unfortunately, judges quickly dismissed most of them. They rendered formalistic interpretations of the law, rejected extemporaneous criminal definitions based on international law, and enforced statutes of limitations and the amnesty. In other words, almost no aspect of the innovative legal vocabulary patiently crafted by Latin America's human rights community to overcome the legal obstacles facing human rights cases has penetrated Brazilian courts (Gonzalez-Ocantos 2016a, chapter 6).

The other emblematic case of rampant impunity is Mexico. One of the most promising aspects of the 2000 democratic transition was President Fox's appointment of a special prosecutor to investigate the massacres and forced disappearances perpetrated during the 'dirty war' of the 1960s and 1970s (Gonzalez-Ocantos 2016a, chapter 5). The FEMOSPP,[20] as the prosecutor's

---

[20] In Spanish FEMOSPP stands for Fiscalía Especializada para la Atención de Hechos Probablemente Constitutivos de Delitos Federales Cometidos Directa o Indirectamente por Servidores Públicos en contra de Personas Vinculadas con Movimientos Sociales y Políticos del Pasado.

office was called, was well-funded and employed a large team of investigators, prosecutors, and historians. It filed at least 15 cases and secured a number of indictments. Unfortunately, however, the prosecutors pursued notoriously deficient strategies, due in part due to the absence of consolidated support structures in civil society, and an alarming lack of technical capacity to investigate complex crimes. For example, prosecutors failed to rely on criminal definitions such as 'forced disappearance', which would have allowed them to circumvent the intractable problem of statutes of limitations.[21] Similarly, in one of the cases they filed genocide charges against a former president even though it was clear that the crimes did not fit this criminal definition. The courts did not help either. Like in Brazil, judges had no command of, and showed no acceptance of, the innovative legal vocabulary exploited elsewhere to carve out a space for criminal accountability amidst expired statutes of limitations and amnesty laws. In the genocide case, for example, the Supreme Court was notoriously out of step with uncontroversial interpretations of international law, declaring that in Mexico genocides are subject to statutes of limitations. All of the indictments were eventually dismissed, and the FEMOSPP was dismantled in 2006, with little to show for it.

1.2 Truth Commissions

Latin American countries have made crucial contributions to the development of another prominent TJ mechanism: truth commissions. According to Hayner (2010: 11–12):

> a truth commission (1) is focused on past, rather than ongoing, events; (2) investigates a pattern of events that took place over a period of time; (3) engages directly and broadly with the affected population, gathering information on their experiences; (4) is a temporary body, with the aim of concluding with a final report; and (5) is officially authorized or empowered by the state.

While courts take a piecemeal, case-by-case approach to 'truth', truth commissions seek to paint a more comprehensive picture, focusing on institutional failures rather than individual responsibilities. Fact-finding and the conclusions drawn from these facts are therefore not necessarily constrained by rules of evidence or criminal procedure. This means that commissions often provide a more amicable environment for victims, and are able to establish and narrate general atrocity patterns, delve into the structural roots of violence, and recommend reforms that strengthen respect for human rights. In addition to their inherent potential for

---

[21] In one case filed after the FEMOSPP was dismantled, prosecutors did rely on the concept of 'forced disappearance', and obtained a 5-year conviction against a former military-intelligence officer in 2009 (Yankelevich 2018).

victim engagement and the promotion of guarantees of non-repetition, truth commissions do not usually face the same political opposition or legal hurdles that characterize judicial struggles. As a result, they are often a suitable alternative when the political space for judicialization remains narrow. The information disseminated by truth commissions sometimes emboldens and legitimizes the demand for trials, widening those narrow windows of opportunity. And if trials eventually take place, judges can find evidence collected by truth commissions extremely helpful.

In what follows I discuss the achievements of truth commissions in Argentina (1983–1984), El Salvador (1992–1993), and Peru (2003). As in the previous subsection, I chose these commissions because they were all influential in the global genealogy of TJ mechanisms. Furthermore, they exemplify the wide range of variation in mandates, conclusions, and effects of truth commissions across three decades of struggles for truth and justice in Latin America. In particular, the cases illustrate possible connections between truth- and justice-seeking efforts, as well as the ways in which truth commissions, like trials, can lead to backlash. I also present a brief account of truth-telling efforts in Mexico, a rare case of spectacular failure. The contrast with the three successful cases helps bring into sharper focus the conditions under which truth seeking is more likely to thrive.

1.2.1 Argentina

Within a week of taking office in December 1983, President Alfonsín created the National Commission on the Disappeared (CONADEP). Like the 1985 ruling against the juntas, the CONADEP played a formative role in the global history of TJ. In fact, the term 'truth commission' did not exist at the time, but gradually took root in Argentina's seminal experience (Sikkink 2008).

The CONADEP's mandate was limited to disappearance cases, with the ultimate goal of locating the victims or their remains. Initially, human rights groups were critical of the initiative. They preferred a parliamentary commission with subpoena powers, but in the end decided to cooperate, transferring troves of information about the crimes. The commissioners relied on these files, plus visits to torture camps and thousands of testimonies gathered throughout the country, as the main sources of evidence. In September 1984 the CONADEP released a report that documented 8,961 disappearances and identified more than 350 clandestine detention centres (CONADEP 1984). While the title of the report was prescriptive ('Never Again'), the content was mainly descriptive – i.e. it produced a thorough and vivid account of the repressive apparatus and its practices, judicial passivity in the face of rights violations, and the human toll of the violence. Importantly, unlike subsequent truth commissions, the CONADEP did not focus on recommending guarantees of non-repetition, or discussing the structural causes of the repressive plan. This was not yet part of the TJ 'script'. Nevertheless, the report had important implications for future TJ efforts.

The commission was a non-judicial body, and as such did not have the prerogative to assign individual criminal responsibility. This limitation notwith-standing, several months into the fact-finding mission the commissioners con-cluded that the best way to proceed was to identify possible perpetrators (Crenzel 2008: 181). The decision promoted a more collaborative relationship with survivors and human rights organizations, and led to the adoption of a quasi-legalistic approach to the inquiry. In practice, this meant that the investigators were at pains to collect evidence that could be admissible in court. They also took great care to organize the documentation in a way that reflected the systematic nature of the repressive plan – for example, filing individual disappearance cases by clandestine detention centre. It is widely recognized that this methodology made judicial accountability efforts much easier once the commission transferred the files to the courts. Interestingly, the commissioners defied the executive's prosecutions policy by sending the files to civilian judges, as opposed to restricting information flows to military courts. While they did not publicly name the perpetrators, all the information was now in the hands of federal judges (Hayner 2010: 94). Broadening the scope of the CONADEP's inquiry not only enabled the swift trial of the junta leaders, but also played a role in the expansion of accountability efforts after 1985. As noted earlier, the surge in indictments led to backlash from the military rank and file, the amnesty laws, and, eventually, the pardons.

In addition to boosting criminal accountability efforts, the CONADEP also contributed to the implementation of monetary reparation policies in the 1990s. The meticulous filing of evidence corresponding to each victim made it easier for families to claim benefits once Congress passed a reparations law in 1994. By contrast, those not named in the report must present new evidence in order to be granted reparations. The scheme was expanded several times over the course of the following 15 years to reach other victims, including those who were forced into exile and the children born in clandestine detention centres.

1.2.2 El Salvador

The Commission on the Truth for El Salvador illustrates the next step in the evolution of global standards and practices associated with truth commissions. In fact, together with Chile's National Commission on Truth and Reconciliation (1990–1991), it was one of the first to feature the word 'truth' in the title. This signalled that the international community was beginning to recognize truth as a right, and truth seeking as part of state duties in the face of mass atrocities. The truth commission was part of the UN-brokered peace agreements between the government and the FMLN, which put an end to a long civil war. Its creation was formally agreed in Mexico City in 1991, prior to the final peace deal of 1992. The parties involved in creating the commission studied the Argentine experience very closely, and concluded that empowering a fact-finding body was a good way to avoid the destabilizing potential of prosecutions. They also took lessons from Chile, which led to a relatively broad mandate: the commission would not only investigate 'serious acts of violence', but would also be tasked with proposing reforms to improve the country's human rights record and reduce the likelihood of future violence. However, unlike the Chilean commission, the drafters decided the staff would be 100 per cent international. This was an attempt to shield the body from politicization and accusations of impartiality in a polarized environment (Ensalaco 1994: 661). The historical importance of the Salvadorean case therefore lies in the fact that it was the first time the international community took full responsibility for running a truth-seeking operation of this kind.

Despite its broad mandate, the commission was given only 8 months to complete the task. The final report, *From Madness to Hope*, was released in March 1993. The commissioners received 22,000 complaints, but zoomed in on 33 emblematic crimes, including the infamous *El Mozote* massacre. They relied on thousands of witness testimonies, documentation provided by human rights organizations, and the help of international forensic experts. One of the main conclusions was that state officials were responsible for 85% of the acts of violence. Crucially, and despite its clear non-judicial mandate, the report made the unprecedented move of publicly naming 40 civilian and military officers allegedly responsible for human rights crimes. In addition, it recommended changes to the judiciary, the criminal code, and the army, and proposed a reparations programme consisting of monetary and symbolic measures. The report emphasized the need to resocialize key institutional actors and entrench a human rights culture.

The report was instantly repudiated by the government and the armed forces, rumours of a military coup included. In response to the naming of alleged perpetrators, Congress swiftly approved a draconian amnesty law 5 days later (Hayner 2010: 102). While the commission never discussed the issue of amnesty provisions, it explicitly recommended against a programme of criminal prosecutions, citing the 'glaring inability of the judicial system either to investigate crimes or to enforce the law' (Betancour, Figuereido, and Buergenthal 1993: 169), an argument that gave additional cover to the proponents of the law. The amnesty law proved extremely resilient, blocking any attempt to successfully judicialize the violence in domestic courts for more than 20 years (Martínez-Barahona and Gutiérrez-Salazar 2016). Despite the lessons that the actors involved in El Salvador's peace process had supposedly learnt from the Argentine case, these developments show that 'truth without justice' can also have a direct impact on political stability. In addition, the trajectory of El Salvador after the release of the report also suggests that there is no necessary connection between truth and justice. In other words, truth commissions may embolden and facilitate accountability efforts, like the CONADEP did in Argentina, but they can also strengthen the resolve of pro-impunity forces.

It is worth noting, however, that the decision to name the perpetrators did have some positive consequences. The peace accords had created an Ad Hoc Commission separate from the truth commission tasked with purging the armed forces. The government was at first reluctant to dismiss officials named in the secret lists submitted by the Ad Hoc Commission, so the truth commission's shaming exercise put decisive pressure on the president. As a result, a series of high-ranking officials were retired. More generally, because the truth commission was part of a broader international reform effort, the government could not pay lip service to the various reform recommendations. In fact, several of the commission's key proposals were implemented surprisingly quickly. For example, the government removed around 200 senior officers from the armed forces. The commission also 'called on the current justices of the Supreme Court to resign' (Ensalaco 1994: 664–665). Within a year, all justices associated with the old regime retired. The procedures to appoint and review lower court judges were also reformed in order to enhance judicial independence. Furthermore, the country brought its code of criminal procedures more in line with human rights standards in 1996 (Hayner 2010: 191).

1.2.3 Peru

According to Hayner (2010), the Peruvian Truth and Reconciliation Commission (CVR) is one of the five strongest truth commissions the world has ever seen. The CVR was established by presidential decree in 2001. Commissioners were tasked with investigating human rights violations during the armed conflict (1980–2000) and contributing to criminal accountability efforts. They were also expected to propose a reparations plan and guarantees of non-repetition. The mandate was therefore exceptionally broad, in part reflecting that, by the early 2000s, the international truth-seeking 'script' had become much more robust. Such a broad mandate was also a function of relatively permissive political conditions following Fujimori's spectacular fall from grace and the resounding defeat of the Shining Path (Gonzalez-Cueva

2004). In this respect, the Peruvian case is different from those of Argentina and El Salvador, where policymakers faced greater constraints or were guided by less ambitious international scripts.

The CVR was in place for 24 months, and it employed hundreds. For many young researchers and activists, this was a truly formative experience. The commission worked closely with local and international institutions to collect and analyse forensic evidence as well as more than 17,000 witness testimonies, especially from victims living in remote and marginalized areas of the country. The commissioners also interviewed some of the alleged perpetrators, including a former president. It was the first truth commission to hold public hearings, allowing it to have a significant impact on public opinion (Gonzalez-Cueva 2004). Using a comprehensive database and the aid of statisticians, the 2003 final report estimated that the conflict resulted in around 70,000 deaths or disappearances. The narrative put emphasis on racism, sexism, and poverty as structural determinants of the violence. It established the existence of 4,600 mass graves, and that 54 per cent and 37 per cent of the deaths were attributable to the Shining Path and the army, respectively. The report is phenomenally long and features in-depth studies of the violence in most regions, as well as thematic chapters discussing how the violence permeated specific groups in society (Hayner 2010).

In addition to the public hearings, the CVR was innovative because of its special focus on contributing to criminal accountability efforts. According to Gonzalez-Cueva (2004: 62), 'at the hearings, victim after victim demanded that the criminals be punished. In the victims' view, only after criminal justice was achieved, would other forms of reparation be asked for and reconciliation attained.' This experience prompted the commissioners to create a Special Investigations Unit charged with preparing criminal cases. In the end, the CVR identified 189 perpetrators (Hayner 2010: 138), and recommended prosecutions in 47 cases, making sure they were representative of the temporal and geographical dynamics of the conflict. Crucially, the CVR appointed a special legal team to prepare a chapter for the final report that explained the international legal basis for prosecutions, and thus improve judicial capacity to prosecute the crimes. According the person in charge of this team, and in contrast with the more defeatist stance of the Salvadorean commission,

> We knew that … we had to expand its original mandate to provide a clear, almost pedagogical interpretation of the Peruvian legal framework in light of international law. We had to make it clear that it was unacceptable and illegal to use legal formalisms and parochial readings of the law to stop the judicialization process.[22]

---

[22] Interview, Lima, 10 March 2010.

This comprehensive effort jump-started a judicialization process that has delivered impressive results, and it is still ongoing. It also demonstrated that although there may not be a necessary link between truth and justice, truth commissions can act in a variety of ways to support criminal accountability. In other areas, however, the CVR was less successful. Most notably, it promoted a large-scale consultation exercise with relevant stakeholders to come up with a reparations programme, and this resulted in an innovative plan focused on development initiatives for marginalized communities ravaged by the violence, as well as on individual monetary reparations. Unfortunately, however, implementation has been fraught with difficulties and painfully slow.

1.2.4 Mexico

President Fox rose to power in 2000, when the PRI lost its first presidential election in 70 years. One of Fox's signature policies was the appointment of a special prosecutor to investigate crimes perpetrated during the 'dirty war'. This decision followed the release of a report by the National Human Rights Commission in 2001, which documented 275 cases of forced disappearance. Fox chose to complement this initial effort with a criminal accountability strategy rather than a truth-seeking one, partly because the PRI strongly opposed the creation of a truth commission. But, once appointed, the special prosecutor made an ambitious interpretation of his mandate and announced that in addition to filing criminal charges his team would produce a report similar to those drafted by truth commissions around the world. This was possible due to the availability of copious amounts of documentation following Fox's decision to declassify key archives. Furthermore, the special prosecutor assembled a team of historians tasked with organizing this information and assisting the investigative efforts (Gonzalez-Ocantos 2016a: 215–216).

Unfortunately, however, the work of the historians was never joined up with that of the prosecutors, with fatal consequences for both truth and justice. Prosecutors opted for looking at each disappearance case individually, paying lip service to the broader context in which the crimes had been perpetrated. This was precisely the contribution that historians could have made to the investigative effort, as demonstrated by the work of other truth commissions. Human Rights Watch warned at the time that 'the investigations of disappearances ... should be based on the study of patterns of violations, and not on isolated incidents' (Seils 2004: I-26). This is because in order to attribute responsibility to those high up in the security apparatus, and to characterize the crimes using international legal categories, it is indispensable to show the systematic nature of the repressive effort and its command structures. But the prosecutors were not trained in the investigation of this type of crime, and, as a result, they were not interested in making use of international legal categories or profiting from the contextual evidence unearthed by the historical team. Their piecemeal approach inevitably generated tensions with the historians, who by virtue of their immersion in the archival material pushed for a more systemic approach and came to realize the power of international legal categories to adequately describe what they saw.

Tensions peaked when the prosecutors heavily modified an initial draft of the report prepared by the historians. Specifically, the prosecutors removed any language that signalled systematicity or mentioned international legal categories. The head of the historical team told the press that 'the list of unreasonable changes was huge, and we felt that they began to treat us as the enemy' (La Jornada, 30 April 2006). As a result of this fallout, someone leaked the original draft, a move that embarrassed the special prosecutor and forced him to spend precious political capital giving excuses. Crucially, this undermined the legitimacy of the truth-telling effort, to the point that the much-awaited report was never officially published.

To my knowledge, the spectacular failure of Mexico's truth-telling effort is unique, but points to a number of important factors behind the success of the other three cases analysed thus far. First, this was not a truth commission with a clear mandate to produce an authoritative account of the past. The truth-seeking effort was always subsidiary to the criminal accountability effort, making it more difficult to amass its own visibility and legitimacy. Second, while the prosecutor showed commitment to the cause when he decided to add a truth-seeking component to his mandate, the historical team was not led by prestigious personalities, as was the case with the other three truth commissions. This prestige is what allowed commissioners in Argentina, Peru, and El Salvador to effectively expand the remit of their fact-finding mission and withstand the political attacks that followed. Third, Mexican investigative efforts were archive-centred, as opposed to being organized around victim testimonies. The latter approach helped truth commissioners in Argentina, Peru, and El Salvador anchor their work in solid structures of social support. Mexico's special prosecutor thus failed to engineer the backing of a critical mass of human rights organizations. As we saw in the Argentine and Peruvian cases, victims provide political insulation, cement officials' commitment to truth, and encourage commissioners to expand their mandates and pursue more ambitious TJ efforts.

2 Power and Norms

What explains Latin America's myriad innovations in the field of TJ? Why is there variation across time and space in TJ outcomes? What explains impunity and silence, as well as breakthroughs in the quest for truth and justice? In this section, I evaluate two influential explanatory approaches: the Huntingtonian and Justice Cascade models.

2.1 Power

The first wave of literature on the determinants of TJ focused on the distribution of political power between outgoing authoritarian actors and incoming democratic elites during and after processes of regime change. Samuel Huntington made the most forceful defence of this analytical approach, which gives primacy to power politics, hence why I call this framework the Huntingtonian Model. Huntington starts his famous discussion of the 'torturer problem' by claiming that 'in actual practice what happened [after transitions] was little affected by moral and legal considerations. It was shaped almost exclusively by politics, by the nature of the democratization process, and by the distribution of political power' (1991: 215). The analysis concludes with the following proposition:

> Officials of strong authoritarian regimes that voluntarily ended themselves were not prosecuted; officials of weak authoritarian regimes that collapsed were punished, if they were promptly prosecuted by the new democratic government ... The popular support and indignation necessary to make justice a political reality fade; the discredited groups associated with the authoritarian regime re-establish their legitimacy and influence. In new democratic regimes, justice comes quickly or it does not come at all (Huntington 1991: 228).[23]

Huntington was not alone in predicting such *political* and *temporal* constraints. Roht-Arriaza (1995: 282) similarly stated that 'measures must be put in place relatively quickly, before the new government loses the widespread legitimacy it enjoys, before the political unity engendered by opposition to the old regime evaporates and apathy sets in, [and] before the old guard can reorganize'.

Other authors built on these foundations. For example, Pion-Berlin (1994: 106) argues that 'political realities dictated that policymakers weigh carefully the costs, benefits, and risks associated with their decisions'. His explanation for variation in outcomes, however, makes a strong case for the importance of

---

[23] While Huntington focuses on prosecutions, he states that 'truth as well as justice was a threat to democracy' (1991: 231), thus implying that similar forces explain the implementation of truth commissions.

presidential leadership. While the balance of power frames the process, the actual decision to prosecute is heavily influenced by presidents' personal experiences with repression and subjective assessments of risk. Pion-Berlin's account thus allows more room for agency, but is still in line with the view that the game of TJ is one that is decided by powerful elites. For example, he downplays factors such as the strength of human rights activism.

Theoretical propositions focused on the role of power and leadership echo arguments advanced during the *normative* debates that took place during the 1980s regarding the desirability of maximalist TJ policies. In *Transitions from Authoritarian Rule*, O'Donnell and Schmitter (1986) advanced maxims of political prudence that in the case of TJ warned of the inevitable conflict between moral imperatives and practical challenges. This work was part of a shift towards agency-based models of democratization, which emphasize the role of judgement in more or less constraining strategic interactions among elites. In rejecting the idea that transitional leaders are actors in a Greek tragedy, hopelessly driven by structural forces beyond their control, they influenced other contributions that discussed how incoming democratic elites should behave during TJ processes. For example, several participants at a conference organized by the Aspen Institute in the late 1980s argued that leaders can indeed shape TJ outcomes, but ought to consider very carefully the reality around them before exercising judgement (Arthur 2009). During the conference, José Zalaquett, former head of Amnesty International's executive board, maintained that 'setting standards which are too rigid and impractical' could be counter-productive (1990: 626). Governments must be prepared to accept trade-offs in terms of whether or not they prosecute widely, selectively, or at all. In his view, the only trade-offs that 'simply cannot be countenanced' are those that relegate truth-telling efforts (Zalaquett 1990: 631). Similarly, Jaime Malamud-Goti, one of Alfonsín's key advisors, noted that prosecutions are 'a messy process' that often suffers from 'sharp political setbacks and constraints – defined, in particular, by the capacity of military members and judges to close ranks and obstruct the process' (Arthur 2009: 351).

These 'realist' recommendations were later countered by more 'idealist' authors. In an influential essay, Diane Orentlicher suggested that prosecutions constitute an international obligation, and that if justified in terms of these higher-order duties, 'they are less likely to be perceived – and opposed as – political revanchism' (1991: 2549). Furthermore, she argued that retribution is essential to consolidate the ethical foundations of democratic institutions and the rule of law (see also Acuña and Smulovitz 1997; Méndez 1997). In an equally famous response essay, Carlos Nino criticized Orentlicher's idealism because it 'does not sufficiently account for the varied and often quite difficult realities successor governments must face ... I doubt the beneficial effects of a general duty which does not take into account those complexities' (1991: 2619).

The realist framework, in both its predictive (e.g. Huntington) and prescriptive (e.g. Zalaquett) versions, finds support in the empirical record. The balance of power in the aftermath of transitions does shape the limits of political possibility. Indeed, the notion that 'the victor tells the tale' squares well with important instances of TJ. The trials in Tokyo and Nuremberg are obvious examples. Similarly, when the Greek junta left power after suffering a military defeat in 1974, human rights abusers were taken to military courts, and matters were settled very quickly. By contrast, after the Spanish negotiated transition (1975–1977), no attempts were made to prosecute those involved in the crimes of Franco's regime. In an important large-N study of the determinants of TJ, Olsen, Payne, and Reiter (2010: 56–57) confirm that 'clean breaks' with the past make trials more likely, although they do not detect an effect on truth commissions.

The contrast between developments in Argentina in the 1980s, on the one hand, and Brazil, Chile, and Uruguay, on the other, also supports Huntingtonian intuitions. Alfonsín won the presidency in 1983 after the juntas suffered a military defeat. Consequently, their power during and after the transition was much reduced in comparison to that of their counterparts in the rest of the Southern Cone. Outgoing dictators in Brazil, Chile, and Uruguay were therefore able to protect themselves from prosecutions. In addition, among all incoming democratic presidents, Alfonsín was the one closest to human rights organizations. His personal preferences and experiences with repression are therefore another factor that explains Argentina's exceptionalism in terms of early TJ outcomes (Pion-Berlin 1994). As Huntington himself noted, backlash against these achievements in the late 1980s can be explained by possible miscalculations regarding the actual political space for ambitious accountability measures, or the corrosive effect of letting the process drag on for several years.

Further afield, during transitions from conflict to peace in Central America, international pressure successfully pushed for truth commissions, but was not enough to promote trials because the domestic balance of power – relative stalemate between belligerent factions in El Salvador and a clear victory for the army in Guatemala – did not favour criminal accountability (Collins 2011; Braid and Roth-Arriaza 2012; Michel 2018). Similarly, the power of the military and the PRI in post-transition Mexico was still significant, limiting the viability of TJ. President Fox's team quickly realized that pushing too far in the direction of accountability for crimes perpetrated during the 'dirty war' risked alienating the PRI's congressional delegation, which they needed to pass legislation. Even though Fox appointed a special prosecutor in 2001, the momentum in favour of TJ languished partly because it lacked more decisive presidential support (Gonzalez-Ocantos 2016a: 225–230). In contrast to all of these cases, the defeat of the Shining Path in Peru, coupled with the collapse of the government that brought about that military victory, opened up much greater space for ambitious truth and justice initiatives that targeted both sides of the conflict (Gonzalez-Cueva 2004).

While definitely not without merits, the Huntingtonian Model does not quite match the protracted story of activism and breakthroughs presented in Section 1. The model's emphasis on political constraints and narrow temporal windows of opportunity very much reflects the anxieties of a time when TJ processes were still highly experimental, leading experts to conclude that TJ was only possible under highly permissive conditions and if policies were implemented swiftly. But we now know that TJ is not a one-shot game, demands for accountability do not simply fade, and processes are fundamentally dynamic. Moreover, adverse political environments do not overdetermine impunity, and hospitable ones do not necessarily guarantee justice. Finally, we also know that the cast of actors involved in TJ processes extends beyond military and political elites.

Some contend that this dynamism should not lead us to discard the central proposition of the Huntingtonian Model, namely that TJ processes are driven by elite-level politics (Lessa et al. 2014). A few scholars, for example, attribute the resurgence of truth and justice initiatives in Latin America in the late 1990s and early 2000s to the rise to power of progressive presidents with electoral incentives to promote TJ, or with a past in human rights activism. Such backgrounds gave these leaders a personal motive and the credibility to champion the cause, (re)open criminal investigations, or launch delayed truth-seeking initiatives (Evans 2007; Karl 2007; Roehrig 2009). The Kirchners in Argentina, who presided over the recent explosion of trials, or the Workers' Party in Brazil, which promoted the country's first truth commission 26 years after the transition, are often referenced to support the argument. The problem with this extension of the Huntingtonian Model is that the continuing focus on elite actors does not explain why the issue of TJ did not simply die out during the intervening years, eventually allowing progressive elites to capitalize on TJ. It also fails to provide an account for why it was possible to actualize such policy preferences years post-transition in some countries but not others. For example, why were Argentine courts able to overcome key legal obstacles such as statutes of limitations or amnesty laws, and thus satisfy a new pro-accountability political consensus, whereas those in Brazil proved incapable or unwilling to do so despite an increasingly permissive political context?

More problematic for the model is that we observe important breakthroughs in countries where the passage of time did not shift the balance of power against pro-impunity forces, or TJ 'spoilers' quickly re-emerged as obstacles for truth and justice. The Huntingtonian Model, with its focus on elite power politics, is not well-equipped to explain these clear departures from elite preferences. Key legal victories in Argentina and especially Chile during the 1990s and early 2000s are a case in point: presidents in both countries were opposed to prosecutions, or at least tried hard to limit their reach, but trials still gained momentum and eventually turned into waves (Collins 2011; Skaar 2011). The trials in Guatemala since 2008 are another good example. As we saw, they occurred amidst the continuing presence of strong elite opposition to TJ (Burt 2016; Michel 2018). And in Peru, courts delivered impressive results over nearly two decades after the 2000 transition, despite the clear relegitimation and re-empowerment of conservative forces following the brief post-Fujimori spring (Gonzalez-Ocantos 2016a: 160–172).

In this sense, one of the key shortcomings of the Huntingtonian Model is that it depicts TJ as a function of a principal–agent relationship in which the powerful dictate outcomes, and courts or truth commissions comply. But the various cases discussed in Section 1 point to the presence of agency loss. Argentine courts during the 1980s orbited away from the president's policy preferences (Acuña and Smulovitz 1997), and so did judges in other countries. Judicial bureaucracies reproduce their own internal cultures, develop institutional missions, and may therefore resist in a corporate fashion outside imperatives to limit accountability. Similarly, despite being given limited mandates by international accords or presidential decrees, truth commissions in Argentina, El Salvador, and Peru quickly reinterpreted their missions, always in expansive ways, and defied their principals. The opposite is also true. Notwithstanding the election of pro-accountability presidents in the 2000s, institutions tasked with delivering TJ sometimes proved unresponsive or highly incompetent. For example, courts in Brazil were not moved at all by the pro-accountability push under the PT, partly because of the persistence of deeply conservative views within the judiciary (Abrão and Torelly 2012). Even in Argentina under the Kirchners, several recalcitrant judges in key courts refused to go along with the strong political momentum in favour of criminal prosecutions, thus obstructing the process (Gonzalez-Ocantos 2014). Overall, this agency loss is one of the reasons why TJ processes acquired a fundamentally dynamic character and transcended transitional moments. It also helps explains puzzling breakthroughs in hostile political environments, as well as wide-ranging variation in outcomes in more hospitable ones.

A related shortcoming of the Huntingtonian Model is that it theorizes TJ with a focus on a very small cast of actors – i.e. domestic military and political elites. Some of the questions left unanswered by the model point to important underlying social processes that transcend elite politics. The presence and continuous mobilization of other actors – namely, human rights movements, foreign governments and institutions, and transnational activists – is partly responsible for the dynamism that characterizes these processes. They keep the issue alive, craft creative legal arguments in order to open or exploit cracks in impunity firewalls, and catalyse agency loss by establishing relationships with judges and truth commissioners. I now turn to a second explanatory framework that incorporates these actors and is thus able to plug some of the gaps in 'power politics' explanations.

2.2 Norms

The second approach brings attention to international norms and social mobilization. These factors are thought to transform state practices vis-à-vis truth and justice during complex transnational processes, and eventually unleash what Kathryn Sikkink (2011) calls a 'justice cascade'. The key insight advanced by this line of research is that TJ is a 'script' that developed over time. It promotes policy templates that turned 'unthinkable' anti-impunity measures into things that states do (or at least debate) as a matter of course when they confront violent pasts. The empirical focus is on how these ideas emerged, and how their diffusion shaped the tactics of contention of, and the balance of power between, pro- and anti-accountability forces. An emphasis on processes of ideational, legal, and discursive construction, as well as on changes in international norms of appropriate state behaviour, endow the framework with the capacity to account for the dynamism of TJ outcomes and the recent convergence towards accountability.

The Justice Cascade approach proposes top-down mechanisms of change with the goal of explaining TJ breakthroughs, especially under adverse local conditions. These scholars contend that the driving force behind struggles for accountability are transnational networks of activists and lawyers who are motivated by personal experiences and principled commitments, and possess specialized knowledge (Sikkink 1993, 2005; Keck and Sikkink 1998; Michel and Sikkink 2013). For example, they promote and design treaties that outline state duties in regard to human rights violations, and use such instruments to develop moral and technical justifications for why states should comply. These efforts put the issue on the agenda of the international community and provide behavioural templates for local elites. As we saw in the case of El Salvador, transnational actors can even play an active role in transitions from conflict to peace, brokering compromises that include the implementation of TJ measures. Individuals plugged into transnational human rights networks also travel to various countries to offer advice, share their experiences, and make recommendations. For example, the Argentine Forensic Anthropology Team (EAAF) has offered crucial technical assistance to several governments and truth commissions in Latin America (Kovras 2017: 84–110).

Transnational networks shape the conditions of possibility for TJ, pressuring, shaming, and persuading reluctant local elites (Risse-Kappen and Sikkink 1999). One prominent mechanism of socialization and behavioural change is the design of international litigation strategies to unlock pathways to truth and justice at the national level (Lutz and Sikkink 2000). In the 1990s, Latin American activists forged alliances with international non-governmental organizations and lawyers, who then filed charges against perpetrators in foreign courts invoking the principle of 'universal jurisdiction' (Lutz and Sikkink 2001). The most famous case was the Pinochet saga of 1998. In fact, the 'Pinochet effect' has become an influential explanation for the momentum behind trials in Argentina and Chile towards the end of the 1990s amidst continued opposition from local elites. During Pinochet's arrest in London, and after his return to Chile, complaints about his responsibility in assassinations and disappearances piled up in Chilean courts, opening the door for many indictments against him and other members of the military regime (Roht-Arriaza 2006; Hilbink 2007; Huneeus 2010). Around this time, trials in abstentia of Argentine military officials in Europe had a similar effect (Lutz and Sikkink 2001). The actions of European judges in all of these cases put the issue of impunity under the spotlight and legitimized the fight against impunity. They also unleashed diplomatic attempts to force governments to clear avenues for accountability in accordance with accepted international standards. For example, Sikkink (2005) documents how Swedish and French officials put pressure on Argentina's President Menem when he visited Europe in the late 1990s.

Human rights organizations also worked transnationally to bring cases to the attention of the Inter-American human rights system (Engstrom 2019), especially the Inter-American Court of Human Rights (hereafter, IACtHR). In response to these litigation efforts, the Court handed down a stream of rulings that called on states to abide by their international responsibilities vis-à-vis truth and justice. Inter-American rulings thus clarified, legitimized, and diffused a legal script that greatly assisted victims and their lawyers in their struggle against impunity at the local level.

A pioneering decision against Honduras in 1988 explained that the state has a 'legal duty to take reasonable steps to prevent human rights violations and to use the means at its disposal to carry out a serious investigation of violations committed within its jurisdiction'.[24] In subsequent decisions, the IACtHR also established a duty to develop judicial structures that ensure the timely investigation and punishment of such crimes,[25] and provided justification for the inapplicability of the *non bis in idem* (double jeopardy) principle when a previous prosecution has not been conducted impartially, especially in military courts or under authoritarian regimes.[26] Furthermore, Inter-American jurisprudence made important contributions to the legal treatment of forced disappearances. The Court sees disappearances as 'a distinct phenomenon, characterized by the multiple and continuous violation of various rights'.[27] According to this view, forced disappearances are crimes that continue to be perpetrated for as long as the whereabouts of the victim remain unknown, implying that statutes of limitations only apply from the moment the body is found. In addition, the refusal to provide information is an essential part of the crime, thus making it possible to extend criminal responsibility to those who participated in planning and covering up the disappearances but didn't directly kidnap or murder the victims. Finally, the lack of information affects not only the immediate victims, but also their relatives. This expands the universe of legally recognized victims and opens the way for claims based on the right to truth as well as the right to justice.[28]

This jurisprudence has been a critical source of creative arguments to remove obstacles for prosecutions, and influenced many of the pathbreaking decisions examined in Section 1. The most consequential Inter-American rulings, however, are those that challenged the legality of amnesty laws. In the celebrated *Barrios Altos* case, the Court argued 'that amnesty dispositions, statutes of limitations and the establishment of exculpatory dispositions that seek to impede the investigation and punishment of those responsible for serious human rights violations … are inadmissible'.[29] This and other similar rulings[30] had corrosive effects on amnesty provisions in Argentina, Chile, El Salvador, Peru, and Uruguay, adding dynamism to TJ processes.[31] Recent changes in the Court's interpretation of amnesty provisions further shaped the conditions of possibility for TJ in more challenging contexts. For example, a concurring opinion by Judge García-Sayán in *El Mozote* v. *El Salvador* (2012) made the case that 'the question of amnesties … requires an analysis that

---

[24] *Velásquez-Rodríguez* v. *Honduras* (1988). Here I focus on the duty to investigate and punish, but the Court has also developed a distinguished body of jurisprudence on reparations.

[25] *Radilla-Pacheco* v. *Mexico* (2009).   [26] *La Cantuta* v. *Peru* (2006).

[27] *Gómez-Palomino* v. *Perú* (2005), paragraph 92.

[28] *Castillo-Páez* v. *Perú* (1997); *Paniagua-Morales and others* v. *Guatemala* (1998).

[29] *Barrios Altos* v. *Peru* (2001), paragraph 41.

[30] *Almonacid* v. *Chile* (2006); *Gelman* v. *Uruguay* (2011); *El Mozote* v. *El Salvador* (2012).

[31] The Court also challenged Brazil's amnesty law, but local judges refused to comply.

provides appropriate criteria for a considered opinion in contexts in which tensions could arise between the demands of justice and the requirements of a negotiated peace in the framework of a non-international armed conflict'. García-Sayán thus softened the Court's position against amnesties, originally developed in cases of crimes perpetrated under military dictatorships. Parties involved in the Colombian peace process explicitly relied on this jurisprudential shift to justify one of the TJ mechanisms embedded in the 2016 peace accords, the Special Jurisdiction for Peace.[32] The accord empowered specialized judges to enforce alternative forms of punishment and reduce sentences if defendants meet a series of conditions. According to one of the main negotiators, new Inter-American jurisprudence provided cover for this controversial measure, which the government considered essential to secure the demobilization of the FARC. It would have been difficult to champion this mix of justice and impunity had the stricter standards against amnesties remained unchanged.[33]

One of the reasons why Inter-American jurisprudence has been so influential in transforming impunity regimes across Latin America, often against the will of domestic political elites, is that the IACtHR went to great lengths to lure domestic judges into a transnational judicial community governed by similar values and juridical standards (Gonzalez-Ocantos 2018). This engineered greater receptivity to innovative Inter-American doctrines and, by implication, to the cases filed by victims in local courts. Aware that unorthodox international standards on truth and justice would not automatically trickle down to national decisions, the IACtHR developed the 'conventionality review' doctrine, which urges judges to rely on Inter-American jurisprudence to evaluate government acts. The Court subsequently engaged in informal networking efforts to communicate directly with national courts, and thus assuage concerns generated by the conventionality review doctrine, in particular those related to the putative supremacy of international law. For example, Uruguayan judges were initially reluctant to accept a ruling that challenged the amnesty law and to recognize their general duty to follow international jurisprudence (*Gelman* v. *Uruguay*, 2011). The IACtHR recognized this problem, and met with the Supreme Court to explain the implications of the *Gelman* decision. Those who witnessed these private conversations claim that the move generated goodwill among local judges, and secured some degree of compliance with international anti-

---

[32] See https://reliefweb.int/sites/reliefweb.int/files/resources/acuerdofinalfinalfinal-1472094587.pdf [accessed 5 June 2019].

[33] Interview, Bogota, 23 August 2016. Despite being enshrined in the peace accords, the Special Jurisdiction for Peace continues to be one of the most contested aspects of Colombia's TJ process, precisely because of these features. For a more extended discussion, see Section 3.

impunity norms in a country otherwise characterized by low levels of success in the area of TJ.[34]

The transnational focus of the Justice Cascade approach is appealing because it helps explain why we observe a certain degree of isomorphism over time in the practical ways in which states have come to deal with demands for truth and justice. In other words, it gives us the analytical tools to understand the gradual regional shift towards accountability. It also presents a more dynamic view of TJ processes, showing how activist networks kept the issue alive, engineering breakthroughs under adverse conditions. These relentless efforts are equally crucial to understand why, under more favourable conditions, some progressive leaders were able to capitalize on the struggle of truth and justice, and effectively promote TJ initiatives many years after the rise of seemingly impenetrable impunity regimes. Furthermore, Justice Cascade scholars highlight the legal and discursive dimension of these struggles. The approach thus offers insights into the empowering effect of well-crafted legal arguments and of the transnational epistemic communities formed in support of those doctrines. These processes of legal construction developed a strong anti-impunity norm, which was used to overcome impunity in several countries. As we saw for the Colombian case, international norm construction efforts also carved out a legitimate space for certain provisions that deviate from strict interpretations of the anti-impunity norm, enabling the implementation of TJ in more challenging contexts. Finally, by focusing on the legal dimension of TJ, the Justice Cascade approach captures the language in which these issues are debated and the terrain where these political battles are fought. Fixating on elite-level 'power politics' risks overlooking an essential feature of the phenomenon – namely, activism and strategic litigation.

Some scholars have criticized the Justice Cascade approach because the timing of international interventions does not always precede important precursors of change at the local level. For example, human rights organizations and judges in Argentina and Chile took important steps in the direction of truth and justice in the early 1990s, several years before the 'Pinochet effect' (Collins 2011; Gonzalez-Ocantos 2016a). Leigh Payne (2008) has also shown that public confessions by high-profile perpetrators spurred intense debates that added momentum to trials before the intervention of international actors. These developments made it possible for subsequent international pressures to catalyse bolder accountability efforts. Relatedly, Justice Cascade explanations are often too 'top down', downplaying

---

[34] Interviews with Inter-American judge (Bogota, 10 August 2016), and the Uruguayan lawyer who brokered the meeting (Montevideo, 12 September 2016). On Uruguay's fraught TJ process and the role of elite obstruction, see Lessa (2012).

important home-grown contributions to TJ (Burt, Fried, and Lessa 2013). For this reason, and mirroring a broader trend in the historiography of human rights norms, scholars now pay more attention to the ways in which actors from the 'south' made the TJ paradigm possible (e.g. Sikkink 2011; 2017, chapter 3). This is in line with the main message I tried to convey in Section 1: that Latin American countries have endogenously produced critical innovations in TJ mechanisms that helped define and expand a global field of practice.

More generally, transnational approaches tend to be less sensitive to lingering cross-country variation in levels of impunity. TJ is a script that needs to be translated and operationalized at the local level in a process that is far from automatic. In fact, this script has not been universally endorsed by state actors, as the cases of Brazil and Mexico demonstrate. Generating political will via international shaming or persuasion, for example, is often not enough. Bureaucrats or judges are not always equipped with the skills, values, or resources to 'do' TJ, and, in turn, respond to intense home-grown or international pressures to comply with human rights standards. Even when these pressures or incentives prove effective, they necessarily exert 'causal' power through the actions of implementation agents that must adapt to changing circumstances in very specific ways. In this sense, like the Huntingtonian Model, the Justice Cascade approach exhibits some degree of voluntarism, failing to fully consider the laborious efforts that make up the causal chain linking pro-accountability pressures to concrete outcomes. To do so, we ought to trace the mechanisms via which state institutions change, or are transformed, to be able to implement unusual and complex policies mandated or encouraged by the global TJ script. In the next section I outline a complementary approach that highlights the importance of domestic institutional change and the infusion of technical capabilities as key variables to understand breakthroughs as well as resistance during TJ process.

3 Building TJ Capabilities

In *Seeing Like a State*, James Scott (1998) explains the development of the modern state as a function of rulers' drive to 'read' and rationalize societies, and thus facilitate order, control, and extraction. Rendering societies legible was not just about capturing a reality that was 'out there', so to speak, but involved creating and imposing categories that in turn refashioned the world: 'a state's cadastral map created to designate taxable property-holders does not merely describe a system of land tenure; it creates such a system through its ability to give its categories the force of law' (1998: 3). Crucially, these efforts depended on much more than the willingness or ability to spend resources. In the case of the cadastral map, in addition to paying for census officials to go around counting and measuring property holdings, the ruler also had to make sure they understood and internalized standardized metrics designed to facilitate taxation rather than other goals. For instance, it would have been counter-productive if equally diligent officers from different regions had measured tracts of land using local or culturally specific metrics ('within earshot', 'a stone's throw', etc.). The modern state and its agents therefore had to start seeing, organizing, and describing the world in a certain fashion to be able to extract efficiently.

The same is true if a state is to 'do' TJ. At some very basic level, TJ is all about capacity building.[35] Re-establishing the rule of law after dictatorship does not happen by decree; it requires investments in institutions to produce changes in the practices of state agents vis-à-vis ordinary people. In the case of countries that experienced civil wars, a primary mission for the state is also to extend its tentacles to areas previously controlled by challengers. But the successful implementation of TJ policies, and achieving the ultimate goal of these policies (i.e. entrenching a human rights culture and a lasting peace), also requires much deeper transformations in the way the state and its agents look at the world around them. Trials, truth commissions, reparations, and guarantees of non-repetition call for a reprogramming of the state: its agents must align actions, priorities, and resource allocation with the obligations associated with the rights to truth, justice, and peace; must be prepared to describe violence using cate-gories that illuminate the significance of certain events; and should see those gruesome realities as urgently compelling courses of action, investigative strategies, and forms of punishment that are different from the routine ways in which the state deals with, say, ordinary crimes. For example, genocides or crimes against humanity are not simply 'out there', but are acknowledged and become official only when state agents document, interpret, and narrate vio-lence using very specific techniques and vocabularies.

TJ involves the development of 'TJ capabilities' via processes of institutional change whereby existing or specially created institutions tasked with dealing with the 'past' (a) incorporate the values of truth, justice, and peace as pillars of their institutional mission; (b) become proficient in various technical aspects of the TJ discourse designed to provide actionable templates for unusual and difficult tasks; and (c) (re)orient routines so that bureaucratic practices do not de facto lead to impunity due to ineffectiveness or lack of prioritization:

---

[35] State capacity is 'the organizational ability to implement governing projects – separate from the political will to deploy it' (Yashar 2018: 108).

- A judge must be able to 'see' a homicide perpetrated in the context of state-sponsored terrorism not just as a regular homicide, but also as a crime against humanity. Learning about international law and adopting this conceptual lens is often crucial to give victims a chance in court, ensuring that statutes of limitations or amnesty laws do not block criminal accountability efforts. Incorporating this vocabulary is also an act of semantic justice that captures the significance of the crime and adds a sense of urgency to the inquiry.
- A prosecutor who finds a mass grave in an area ravaged by civil war should not just 'see' an unfortunate collection of dead bodies that will join the queue in an already packed docket. Instead, the reflex reaction should be to 'see' a reality that requires immediate and highly specialized forensic treatment to preserve and recover evidence, and in the process, affirm society's right to truth.
- A researcher tasked with rummaging through a military archive as part of a national truth-telling effort must be able to orient her work towards the quest for patterns and general dynamics, rather than merely obsess over document-ing the fate of specific individuals. This macro-level perspective is the key to 'seeing' systemic crimes and understanding the root causes of violence.
- A police reform effort with the aim of instituting guarantees of non-repetition in the aftermath of an armed conflict must focus on remaking the values that guide the work of the institution. Where a policeman used to 'see' an enemy, he should now 'see' a citizen; where he used to 'see' an unquestionable order to mass murder, he should now 'see' an affront to his institutional mission.

To be sure, the political will of domestic elites or transnational activism can play an important role in producing these transformations in the way institu-tions see the world, process facts, and instinctively react to them. Presidential decisions to launch a truth commission, funnel scarce resources to a reparations programme, or reform the police obviously help. So does the availability of a global legal script that orients and legitimizes unorthodox juridical practices in the context of human rights trials or the creation of robust fact-finding bodies. But as I discussed in Section 2, these factors are often not sufficient. This is because doing TJ is not only expensive or unprecedented; it is technically challenging for those tasked with implementation. The state requires agents with a host of highly specialized skills, including expertise in forensic science, statistics, sociology, the psychology of trauma, and interna-tional human rights law. In addition to acquiring these capabilities through arduous learning processes, state agents also need to undergo a revolution in their values and commitments. TJ is hard, time consuming, and risky. As a result, those tasked with implementation must be prepared to go the extra mile; rigidly sticking to their terms of reference won't serve the cause very well. For instance, information about military operations and repressive structures is rarely forthcoming because those responsible for state crimes tend to protect their own. Gathering incriminating evidence therefore cannot be a passive exercise centred around formal information requests; it requires unusual creativity and zeal, and stepping outside bureaucratic comfort zones. Collecting witness testimonies from victims can also be difficult. Truth commissioners and judicial authorities must spend months painstakingly building trust with communities whose lives were destroyed by the same state that now seeks to engage them. This often requires extraordinary coordination with translators, therapists, and anthropologists.

The point is that the implementation of TJ depends on the presence of skilled and committed state agents who are ready to take on unprecedented and difficult tasks. This means that even if we accept that domestic and international political pressures take the driver's seat in TJ processes, shaping the state's willingness to invest in such capabilities and the ensuing implementation levels, it is still important to describe and understand how the state is refashioned to translate political will into policy outputs through complex and multifaceted sequences of institutional learning, adaptation, and change. An eye on the role of institutional change and the creation of TJ capabilities also helps explain why we observe breakthroughs in unlikely places, especially in contexts where the political class staunchly opposes TJ. When new skills and ways of seeing the world develop, state agents internalize a commitment to novel routines and standards that may inspire rebellions against their principals. If this happens, TJ can be decoupled from broader political dynamics and shielded from backlash. For example, if a judge is persuaded by human rights organizations, and thus comes to think in terms of international legal categories and internalizes a commitment to fulfil the state's international responsibilities, it is more likely that he will find new amnesty provisions unacceptable and become less susceptible to pressures to stop the investigations.

Several truth commission reports in Latin America clearly foresaw a litany of implementation challenges, and called for the development of TJ capabilities that would enable these processes to move forwards, create the necessary bureaucratic autonomy to shield them from backlash, and eventually routinize respect for human rights. Argentina's *Nunca Mas* innovated by using part of the report to shine a light on the institutional deficits that enabled state-sponsored terrorism, especially inside the judiciary. Many of these practices were intentional, but others reflected deeply ingrained legal routines that produced a structural bias against the protection of human rights (Hayner 2010: 106). The final report of Peru's CVR also showed that during the internal armed conflict, formalistic and antiquated legal routines led judicial actors to completely neglect their role as protectors of fundamental rights:

> The judiciary lacked a real capacity to act, or what is even worse, did not have the will to act in defence of the constitutional order . . . [It became] an agent of violence against persons, either because – structurally – judicial operators were constrained by the organization of the judiciary and by ineffective norms, or because those same operators acted in such a way that they left citizens, whose rights they must defend, in a state of destitution (Comisión de la Verdad y Reconciliación 2003: vol. III, ch. VI, 249–250)

Importantly, the report made it clear that Peruvian judicial actors ignored their duty to enforce checks and balances, protect individual rights, and investigate serious violations because of the lack of adequate training in the field of 'constitutional law and the lack of awareness of international human rights instruments' (Comisión de la Verdad y Reconciliación 2003: vol. II, ch. II, 255).

Similarly, El Salvador's Commission for the Truth documented judicial failures in every major instance of human rights violations during the civil war. The problem, commissioners argued, was more than just a bias in favour of conservative interests or counter-insurgency tactics; the problem was rooted in deeper institutional deficits: 'What is ironic is that the web of corruption, timidity and weakness within the judiciary and its investigative bodies greatly impeded the effective functioning of the judicial system even where crimes attributed to FMLN were involved' (Betancour, Figuereido, and Buergenthal 1993: 163). Based on these observations, the report explicitly recommended against judicializing human rights violations; the state simply lacked key TJ capabilities in the form of knowledgeable and committed judges. It did, however, promote a series of institutional changes aimed at enhancing the competence of judicial and security bureaucracies, hoping that prosecutions might be possible in the future. The commissioners put special emphasis on reforming processes of judicial and military training so that judges, prosecutors, and armed officers would develop behavioural routines conductive to the instinctive and routine enforcement of fundamental rights.

Finally, the IACtHR has also raised awareness of TJ capability deficits. As I discussed in Section 1, part of the explanation for why Mexico failed to provide a modicum of truth and justice to victims of past human rights violations has to do with the lack of judicial investigative capacity and knowledge of relevant international law. In *Radilla* v. *Mexico* (2009) the IACtHR reminded the state that in order to fulfil its international obligations it needed a competent judicial bureaucracy, and ordered the implementation of a pedagogical intervention designed to retrain judges:

> The State shall implement . . . a) programs or permanent courses on how to
> analyse the jurisprudence of the Inter-American Human Rights System . . .;
> b) a training program . . . addressed to agents . . . who have jurisdiction in the
> investigation and prosecution of [forced disappearances] in order to provide
> those officials with the necessary legal, technical, and scientific skills to
> comprehensively evaluate the phenomenon of forced disappearance.
> Specifically, in this type of cases the authorities in charge of the investiga-
> tion shall be trained on the use of circumstantial evidence, indicia, and
> presumptions, the assessment of the systematic patterns [etc.].[36]

The kind of institutional change needed for TJ can come about abruptly – for
example, via draconian purges of relevant institutions or the creation of specialized agencies – but it can also take place gradually and incrementally. This
impetus for change, in turn, can come from a variety of sources. It may be pushed
from the top by politicians, international courts, or truth commissions; engineered
from below by civil society; or assisted by international experts. It may even
result from the initiative and 'mission creep' of entrepreneurs working within
judicial, forensic, or security agencies. After all, most bureaucracies tend to
'evolve in ways not intended by their creators' (Barnett and Finnemore 2004:
41). Motives for doing so may range from intra-agency power jockeying to
generational change. Given this diversity in processes, actors, and mechanisms,
developing a fully fledged theory of institutional change and TJ capability-
building is beyond the scope of this monograph. Instead, I will rely on three
short case studies to illustrate how TJ capability-building works in practice under
a variety of conditions.

I will discuss how human rights organizations in Argentina were instrumental
in diffusing knowledge of international law among judicial actors, leading to
important breakthroughs despite political opposition to TJ during the 1990s.
Later on, and despite the presence of a supportive political environment, further
institutional innovations introduced by top judges made the trial wave of the
2000s logistically possible. The Guatemalan case of TJ capability-building is
different in that it took place under a much more hostile political environment
and with a lower baseline level of state capacity. These obstacles notwithstanding, international actors and home-grown judicial leaders were able to
strengthen the bureaucratic autonomy of the prosecution service and the courts,
with important consequences for the viability of justice efforts. Finally, an
overview of the Colombian peace process illustrates how TJ capabilities are
also crucial for national actors in need of avoiding clashes between specific TJ
mechanisms and international norms. More generally, the discussion of the

---

[36] *Radilla* v. *Mexico* (2009), paragraphs 347–348.

Colombian case showcases the enormous challenge of reforming the state so that it can re-orient its structures, practices, and priorities to 'do' TJ.

3.1 Argentina

In the early 1990s, after the initial momentum in favour of TJ had ended, Argentine human rights NGOs realized that in order to stand a chance in court they had to resocialize judicial personnel in federal courts so that they could 'see' human rights cases through the lens of international law. Any attempt to prosecute and punish would languish in the face of amnesty laws and statutes of limitations unless judges were trained in the use of a series of unorthodox legal arguments. To do so, victim organizations mounted pedagogical interventions that targeted key judges and prosecutors. The following is a passage from a 1992 funding application submitted by the executive director of CELS, a leading Argentine NGO, to the International Commission of Jurists. It shows that human rights activists understood impunity partly as a problem of capability deficits:

> [The] goal is to analyze the use of international and regional human rights conventions ... This analysis will include a study of the relevance [of international law] and the objections and obstacles that oppose it ... Judges and lawyers, and even universities, scholars and legal journals frequently ignore [international legal obligations], depriving citizens of the rights and protections they safeguard. For this reason, CELS deems it convenient to organize a regional seminar that brings together legal scholars, judges, lawyers, university professors and advanced law students ... [The meeting] will constitute the first step of a movement that will translate into workshops, seminars, research, publications and judicial rulings.[37]

Elsewhere, I've shown how this kind of pedagogical intervention built judicial capacity and willingness to accept and handle TJ cases, leading to key legal victories in the late 1990s and early 2000s (Gonzalez-Ocantos 2016a). The intervention of NGOs such as CELS equipped judicial actors with the skills and motives to defy narrow limits of political possibility at a time when the executive branch remained opposed to opening up a space for prosecutions. Thanks in part to these victories and the baggage of knowledge and experience accumulated during the proceedings, courts were later on able to set in motion an ambitious programme of criminal prosecutions. Similar waves of pedagogical activism also took place in Peru after the 2000 transition, enabling many judicial victories. In countries such as Brazil, Mexico, and Uruguay, by contrast, victim groups failed to incubate professionalized legal teams, and therefore never

---

[37] Letter from CELS to ICJ, 6 July 1992.

managed to engineer this kind of judicial commitment to criminal accountability.

In order to deliver the trial wave of the 2000s, however, the Argentine judiciary had to adapt further. The question was no longer how to internalize international legal standards, but how to meet the logistical challenge of prosecuting thousands of defendants and holding dozens of trials. This is because Argentina did not create specialized courts for TJ; instead, it relied on existing structures to process the avalanche of human rights cases. Time was of the essence: victims had already waited too long, and defendants were getting old. The good news was that unlike the 1990s and early 2000s, when top federal courts were controlled by judges opposed to or indifferent to TJ, the Supreme Court and other high criminal courts were now staffed with individuals committed to truth and justice, and ready to push for the transformations in bureaucratic routines and practices needed to complete the job. As a result, while civil society actors were the primary engine behind the first stage of institutional change, judicial leaders were at the forefront of a second moment of successful adaptation.

Despite the decisive shift in the balance of power in favour of pro-accountability actors during the Kirchner presidencies (2003–2015), which among other things made possible the aforementioned personnel changes in top courts, there were still a series of bureaucratic hurdles that caused delays and huge variations in judicial outcomes across provincial jurisdictions (Gonzalez-Ocantos 2014). The Supreme Court did two things to ensure that a lack of prioritization did not de facto lead to impunity and, consequently, a more uniform trial rate throughout the country. First, it created an inter-branch commission to identify bottlenecks and offer technical assistance. Together with the appointment of a specialized team of prosecutors within the Procuración General de la Nación, this enabled central judicial authorities to intervene in jurisdictions where judicial capacity was lacking. Interventions in federal courts with jurisdiction over provinces such as Chaco, Mendoza, and Salta proved instrumental in infusing TJ capabilities and changing the trajectory of the docket.

Second, the Supreme Court issued a series of instructions to lower courts with the goal of reorienting decision-making routines and revising inadequate procedural standards. Such behavioural and regulatory changes were deemed necessary to enable and commit courts to 'do' TJ in a timely manner. The directives called attention to judges' international responsibility to prioritize cases of crimes against humanity, and highlighted the importance of avoiding delays produced by an excessively formalistic interpretation of procedural rules. It also encouraged the relevant authorities to implement urgent logistical measures, such as the creation of new courts with jurisdiction in the city of Buenos Aires, where the docket was particularly packed, or renting out new spaces so that Federal Oral Tribunals could conduct more trials simultaneously.[38] This prompted the Court of Cassation, the highest criminal court in the land, to issue a more specific set of instructions. It urged judges to minimize paperwork when transferring case files during the various stages of appeal, enforce shorter deadlines for notifications and appeals, apply stringent relevance criteria when deciding what evidence to admit, and avoid spending precious trial time reading passages from documents produced during the investigation phase. Crucially, the court also instructed judges to avoid the duplication of witness testimonies in similar cases, and declared the admissibility of recordings or transcripts from previous trials.[39]

These and other efforts to change institutional practices enabled a massive logistical undertaking amidst poor infrastructure and inadequate routines, translating political momentum in favour of prosecutions into concrete outcomes. The intervention of high court judges also operationalized abstract international duties enshrined in the global TJ script, providing lower courts with a clear behavioural template that legitimized deviations from customary practice in order to speed up proceedings and apply human rights standards. In so doing, they transformed the way judges perceived human rights cases. But what is really fascinating about the Argentine experience with TJ capability-building is that it supported a relentless process of jurisprudential innovation.[40] Thanks to the entrepreneurship of litigants and top judges, and the resulting exposure to human rights cases, enhanced knowledge of international sources of law, and heightened sense of urgency to process the docket, when new facts about state-sponsored terrorism enter the field of vision of Argentine courts during trial proceedings, judges are inclined to 'read' these facts in a different light. This has led to an expansion in the types of violations that judges place under the category of 'crimes against humanity', with important implications for the scope of the trial wave.

The evolution of the treatment of gender violence in clandestine detention centres helps illustrate how changes in the way judges 'see' cases of state repression can catalyse impressive jurisprudential achievements.[41] Under normal circumstances, prosecutions for sexual assault present numerous challenges and require a special approach to victim testimonies. When dealing with similar

---

[38] Available at www.csjn.gov.ar/documentos/descargar/?ID=29471 [accessed 8 May 2019].

[39] Available at www.oas.org/juridico/PDFs/mesicic4_arg_acordada1-12.pdf [accessed 8 May 2019].

[40] For a catalgoue of jurisprudential innovations, see www.fiscales.gob.ar/wp-content/uploads/2018/03/Lesa-Compendios-2017.pdf [accessed 8 May 2019].

[41] For details of the jurisprudence discussed below, see www.fiscales.gob.ar/wp-content/uploads/2014/08/Delitos-sexuales-y-terrorismo-de-Estado.pdf [accessed 9 May 2019].

crimes perpetrated more than 30 years ago, these challenges are magnified. Applying routine evidentiary and procedural standards almost certainly obscures the presence of gender violence, and guarantees impunity. In fact, according to Balardini, Oberlin, and Sobredo (2011), Argentine judicial actors were initially ill-equipped to deal with sexual assault in the context of human rights trials, and consequently failed to see or appreciate the gender dimension of state repression.

In 2010, a court in the Province of Buenos Aires showed signs that such difficulties could be overcome: the judges issued the first conviction for sexual violence in a forced disappearance case. In the meantime, the special team of prosecutors created within the Procuración General de la Nación recognized the technical challenges presented by sexual crimes, and prepared a brief that sharpened, and further diffused, a sophisticated template to facilitate the detection and legal treatment of gender violence. They also issued a directive urging judicial actors to apply the template.[42] Appellate courts in Mendoza and Tucuman built on these guidelines. They concluded that sexual crimes must be seen as a key component of the repressive effort, rather than as isolated excesses by individual perpetrators and therefore orthogonal to TJ. They linked this interpretation to the notion of mediate authorship, a move that allowed the judges to convict high-ranking officers for rapes perpetrated by the rank and file. Several other judges have since made the case that sexual assaults constitute crimes that need to be singled out and punished separately from others such as torture. In their view, justice is incomplete if authorities adopt a non-gender perspective. They have also argued that in the context of state-sponsored terrorism, sexual assaults should be labelled crimes against humanity. Interestingly, judges sometimes make these arguments even when victims do not file specific charges for sexual assault. This is because, armed with a new institutional lens, itself the product of a series of capability-building efforts, courts are now programmed to read the testimonies of female (and male) survivors in a different light, spotting previously obscured dimensions of the repressive effort and feeling the urgency to produce an official response that elevates the status of certain case facts.

Developments such as these reflect an extremely expansive understanding of the duty to prosecute and punish – one that goes beyond the minimum requirements to comply with international standards or abide by a pro-accountability political consensus. Such progressive bureaucratic dispositions contrast, for example, with those of the Chilean judiciary. As we saw in Section 1, Chilean judges do not even hold uniform views about the status of dictatorship-era

---

[42] See www.derechos.org/nizkor/arg/doc/abusos.html [accessed 9 May 2019].

crimes as crimes against humanity, let alone the importance of prosecuting a wide range of crimes, including gender violence or crimes perpetrated by civilian allies of the regime. In some cases, they are also prepared to apply lenient sentencing criteria. This is arguably because the Chilean judiciary was never subject to bottom-up or endogenous processes of institutional change as robust as those seen in Argentina. The institutional lens through which courts see human rights cases has therefore not been sharpened enough to produce consistent and exemplary bureaucratic responses. While well-organized and persistent, Chilean human rights organizations were always more reactive than proactive in their quest for justice (Collins 2011). Similarly, the upper echelons of the judicial bureaucracy remain more conservative and have not adopted the same leadership role as their Argentine counterparts (Hilbink 2007).[43] Such differences in bottom-up and top-down TJ capability-building may explain variation in the scope of trial waves in two otherwise successful cases.

3.2 Guatemala

Guatemala is notorious for having a state apparatus incapable of performing basic functions, including the administration of justice (Yashar 2018: 168–171). Judicial operators are badly trained and resource poor. For example, the system relies on international cooperation to carry out essential forensic tests (Michel 2018: 82–83). The presence of drug-trafficking organizations and clandestine security forces further fuels prosecutorial paralysis because investigating serious crimes invites huge personal risks. According to Michel, 'between 2005 and 2011, more than twenty-five prosecutors, judges, and judges' clerks were killed' (2018: 85). In the absence of judicial capacity, with human rights abusers still at large, and a deeply entrenched oligarchic military-political establishment, it is nothing short of a miracle that Guatemala has been able to contribute to the 'justice cascade'.

After years of impunity following the peace accords, and a series of failed attempts to replicate the 'Pinochet effect' via international litigation efforts (Roht-Arriaza 2006, chapter 7), the tide started to turn circa 2008. Since then, Guatemalan courts have handed down a number of convictions in high-profile, and extremely complex, cases of human rights violations perpetrated during the civil war (Burt 2016). These efforts survived the backlash against Ríos-Montt's conviction, and continue to haunt the conservative establishment to the present day. Part of the explanation for these puzzling developments has to do with processes of TJ capability-building spearheaded by international and local

---

[43] For a discussion of how a more proactive approach by Chilean victims might be changing judicial capacity to deal with gender violence, see Collins (2018: 38–39; 62–63).

players, which equipped judges and prosecutors with the necessary skills and commitment to deliver justice.

A combination of civil society activism and international pressures led to the establishment of the UN-sponsored International Commission Against Impunity in Guatemala (CICIG) in 2006. The CICIG was set up to 'support and assist domestic justice institutions in the investigation and prosecution of [organized crime and] strengthen the weak judicial system' (International Crisis Group 2011: i). While the mandate specifically excluded the investigation of international crimes (i.e. those related to the armed conflict), capacity-building efforts by CICIG had important spillover effects in that area.

In many ways, the story of the CICIG in Guatemala is one of bureaucratic 'mission creep'. For example, in addition to gradually expanding the payroll to include more international and local staff, the CICIG promoted the creation of a team of local prosecutors tasked with supporting its work. As the International Crisis Group (2011: 7) notes, this opened up the possibility to 'institutionalize important practices learned through regular interactions' and 'for national actors, within and outside the judicial system, to share in CICIG's activities and appropriate its objectives'. The commission also promoted training for prosecutors and the police, as well as changes in judicial selection processes. Additionally, it filed complaints against 'non-cooperative, obstructionist and corrupt officials from multiple institutions' (International Crisis Group 2011: 8). These efforts further contributed to personnel changes and capacity building. Finally, it lobbied for the creation of 'high risk' courts devoted to cases of macro-criminality, including human rights violations. According to the Open Society (2015: 5), since 2009 such cases 'have used these specialized courts, ensuring greater judicial independence, heightened expertise, and greater protection for the judges and other participants'.

After the CICIG successfully lobbied for the appointment of Claudia Paz y Paz, a prestigious lawyer and human rights defender, as Attorney General in 2010, these productive synergies with local judicial actors intensified (Brett 2016: 292). In fact, 'the slowly increasing quantity of criminal prosecution is in part due to the new investigative rigor of the public prosecutor's office under [her]' (Braid and Roht-Arriaza 2012: 194). Kemp (2014: 156) similarly credits Paz y Paz for 'reorganizing and professionalizing' the public prosecution service. One of the ways in which Paz y Paz's leadership transformed institutional routines was the adoption of a victim-centred approach to criminal investigations in human rights cases. This strengthened prosecutors' 'capacity to build cases through witness testimony' (Burt 2016: 146). After years of inaction, during which judicial actors had done little to launch professional investigations and NGOs had acted as substitutes for the state (Michel 2018), the ability to move fast depended on openness to the expertise of human rights lawyers, and the wealth of evidence already collected and pre-analysed by civil society organizations. In many ways, transforming institutional practices vis-à-vis victims was a way to import investigative capacity. Burt (2016: 159) also credits Paz y Paz with furthering TJ capabilities via the introduction of protocols for the investigation of sexual crimes – a central aspect of violence during the armed conflict and a pillar of the genocide case against Ríos-Montt. Much like in Argentina, the focus was on the legal treatment of sexual crimes under international law, safeguards against re-victimization, and witness protection.

As Brett (2016: 294) notes in relation to the Ríos-Montt trial, judicial behaviour reflected 'important advances in capacity-building', particularly regarding the use of 'effective investigative techniques, application of international law, and formulation of solid bodies of evidence for complex criminal cases'. The success stories made possible by these new TJ capabilities produced demonstration effects that emboldened judicial actors further down the line. When TJ capabilities emerge, and bear their fruits, judges and prosecutors develop feelings of efficacy and security in respect of the pursuit of new institutional missions, and are more likely to participate in risky acts of defiance. The threat that enhanced bureaucratic capacity and agency loss pose to those who favour impunity is evidenced by the Guatemalan establishment's refusal to extend Paz y Paz's tenure beyond 2014, the president's decision to terminate the CICIG in 2019,[44] and current attempts to pass a comprehensive amnesty to stop ongoing prosecutions. In other words, elites can no longer assume that judicial acquiesce and ineffectiveness will protect their interests. It remains to be seen whether efforts at TJ capability-building effectively entrenched new values and commitments capable of withstanding such virulent backlash, or produced only feeble and superficial transformations. The fact that institutional changes were introduced over a relatively short period of time, and in a top-down fashion, rather than gradually and organically from below (e.g. via pedagogical interventions orchestrated by NGOs), might not bode well for the future of TJ in Guatemala.

3.3 Colombia

In 2016, the Colombian government signed a peace accord with the FARC, putting an end to a long civil war. The accord includes agreements on a rural reform initiative to tackle issues of land inequality; a policy to combat drug trafficking; and the demobilization, reincorporation, and political participation

---

[44] The Constitutional Court overturned the president's decision. There were calls to impeach the judges following the ruling. At the time of writing, the continuity of the CICIG hangs by a thread.

of the FARC. On the issue of TJ, the accord created a truth commission with a broad mandate, an agency to search for the disappeared, and the Special Jurisdiction for Peace (SJP). The latter is a judicial body charged with processing cases of serious human rights violations, and, most innovatively, it is entitled to apply reduced sentences and alternative forms of punishment in cases where combatants admit responsibility for the crimes.

According to a report issued in April 2019, 69 per cent of the commitments listed in the accords have been implemented to varying degrees.[45] This figure is impressive, especially considering the strength of domestic political opposition to the agreements. In October 2016, for example, voters rejected the peace accord in a referendum. Critics, including former President Uribe (2002–2010), especially trashed the SJP, which they deemed conducive to impunity for FARC members. The result triggered a new round of negotiations. Congress finally approved a modified version of the accords in November 2016. To make matters worse, Uribe's proxy candidate won the presidency in August 2018, meaning that an administration that is deeply sceptical of, and has promised to drastically change, the accord will oversee the bulk of the implementation process. Public opinion also remains overwhelmingly sceptical (Albarracín and Gamboa 2017).

In line with Huntingtonian and Justice Cascade explanations, the signing of the accord, the adoption of ambitious TJ mechanisms, and what for the time being looks like a high implementation rate are partly the result of President Santos's (2010–2018) strong commitment to peace, as well as of the support provided by a host of international and civil society actors throughout.[46] An exclusive focus on the role of powerful elites and international support, however, risks obscuring the importance of TJ capabilities and institutional change in the process. The Colombian state had to be partially refashioned in order to fulfil the aspirations enshrined in the accord. To illustrate this point, I will discuss two aspects of the creation of the SJP, the flagship TJ mechanism. First, I will show how the presence of strong TJ capabilities in the Colombian Constitutional Court (CCC) was important for the sustainability of what was from the start a very controversial initiative. This represents an instance in which international human rights norms clashed with a local TJ mechanism, severely undermining the viability of the SJP. The clash was in part resolved by

---

[45] See https://kroc.nd.edu/assets/316152/190409_pam_media_advisory_final.pdf [accessed 5 June 2019].

[46] The fate of the fledgling peace will also be determined by elite factors, especially the levels of restraint displayed by the new government. At the time of writing, for example, the SJP's refusal to acquiesce to a US extradition order against a FARC commander accused of involvement in drug trafficking has reinvigorated opposition to the deal, and is testing the staying power of this key component of the accord. See www.insightcrime.org/news/analysis/jesus-santrich-case-epicenter-colombia-peace-process/ [accessed 5 June 2019].

the CCC's skilful and credible juridical interpretations of the state's international obligations. Second, I will analyse the massive logistical undertaking that building a new judicial body from scratch entailed, especially one that could 'do' what the accord promised to do. These efforts show TJ capability-building at work.[47]

Government officials believed that the FARC would only agree to demobilize if the accord made it possible for them to avoid prison. As a result, the SJP provides that perpetrators who confess serious crimes can potentially evade jail sentences. According to Hillebrecht, Huneeus, and Borda (2018: 280), the accord thus 'advances an understanding of TJ less punitive than most knowledgeable observers would have deemed allowable'. Indeed, when in 2012 Congress debated the Legal Framework for Peace, a statute that laid the foundations of what would become the SJP, Human Rights Watch pushed for 'key modifications to the bill that would allow Colombia to pursue peace efforts without violating the basic rights of victims of war crimes and crimes against humanity'.[48] More importantly, the International Criminal Court (ICC) also looked at the initiative with suspicion. In 2005, the ICC prosecutor had opened a preliminary investigation into possible international crimes perpetrated during the armed conflict. The threat of this preliminary phase evolving into an actual case before the ICC as a result of a sub-standard TJ framework cast a shadow over the peace negotiations (Hillebrecht, Huneeus, and Borda 2018: 293). In fact, in a series of private letters to the CCC at a time when the justices were examining the constitutionality of the Legal Framework for Peace, the ICC prosecutor warned of this possibility if the peace accord did not comply with strict interpretations of international anti-impunity norms. The right-wing opposition to the accords also demanded compliance with these principles in order to avoid impunity for FARC members.

The presence of TJ capabilities – specifically, the fluency of high-level bureaucrats in the language of international human rights and criminal law – helped the Colombian state navigate these constraints and produce a peace accord that strikes an unusual balance between peace, truth, justice, and reconciliation under the most challenging circumstances. This is true for key diplomats and government officials (Hillebrecht, Huneeus, and Borda 2018: 311), but most importantly, I would argue, for the CCC.

---

[47] There are also examples in which capability deficits undermined the process. The government's inability to effectively reclaim territories formerly controlled by the FARC – a failure that has led to a spike in targeted assassinations of social leaders and former FARC combatants (over 500 since 2016) – is a clear illustration of how state capacity plays a strong conditioning role during the implementation phase.

[48] See www.hrw.org/news/2012/05/31/colombia-amend-legal-framework-peace-bill [accessed 6 June 2019].

Just as it had done in 2006 in relation to the Justice and Peace Law (Rowen 2018: 97–98), which created a similar justice framework to encourage the demobilization of right-wing paramilitaries, in 2013 the CCC ruled on the constitutionality of the Legal Framework for Peace. In so doing, it directly engaged the objections put forward by anti-impunity 'purists'. As one clerk told me, 'we had to fine-tune constitutional law and put it in line with international law because of the ghost of the ICC.'[49] Another was more candid: 'There was an instrumental use of international law as an umbrella to protect the peace negotiations.'[50] In a phenomenally long ruling (C-579/13), the justices put these tools to work, and proposed an interpretation of the TJ framework (plus a few amendments) that ensured compatibility with international legal standards without undermining political viability. The fact that over the years the CCC has developed a global reputation as a source of groundbreaking jurisprudence on fundamental rights, a bridge-builder between domestic and international law, and a key interlocutor of the IACtHR[51] enhanced the authority and credibility of this interpretation, and managed to appease potential 'spoilers' such as the ICC (Anton 2018). This same credibility turned the CCC into an effective mediator between pro- and anti-accord factions at key junctures of the implementation phase. The CCC uses its TJ capabilities to solve complicated questions with answers that are compatible with international law, but also with the narrow limits of political possibility shaped, on the one hand, by the threat that the FARC might abandon its commitment to peace if severe punitivism prevails, and, on the other, that the right might step up its obstructionist tactics should the ex-guerrilla be treated too softly or former military men too harshly.[52]

Once the legal space for an initiative of this kind was cleared, and the accords were signed, the SJP had to be created. The state faced the challenge of building a new branch of government, one with a very specific outlook and set of skills. In order to fulfil the promise of the accords, the SJP had to adopt a specific institutional lens through which to 'see' the past, and be able to perform unusual tasks. The SJP had to invent its own rules of procedure, oversee a huge annual budget, process thousands of complaints and investigate complex crimes, understand the history of a convoluted civil war, navigate the dual worlds of international and domestic law, and manage a complicated relation with the establishment and the public. Crucially, the SJP had to be able to do all of this in

---

[49] Interview, Bogota, 29 August 2016.   [50] Interview, Bogota, 18 August 2016.
[51] For example, it is the Latin American court that most regularly cites the IACtHR (Gonzalez-Ocantos 2018).
[52] For example, the CCC appeased conservative critics by watering down a provision that would have required civilian perpetrators to appear before the SJP (C-674/17). The CCC will also most likely settle the controversy discussed in n. 45.

line with the key goal of the accords: consolidate a transition to peace whilst (a) respecting victim rights and the due process rights of defendants, and (b) adopting a perspective that is mindful of the differential impact of the conflict across the territory as well as of the gender and ethnic dimension of the violence.

In order to fulfil this mission, and in a very short period of time, the SJP set up an intricate bureaucracy, consisting of multiple tribunals and a variety of units that provide legal, investigative, and administrative support throughout the country. For example, to make sure that the SJP has in-built capabilities to 'see' violence patterns in ways that illuminate the differential impact of the conflict on women and ethnic minorities, it created 'gender' and 'ethnic' committees that oversee the work of the entire institution. Moreover, the unit tasked with investigating cases in which there are no perpetrator confessions is equipped to provide assistance to victims and has dedicated sub-units for cases of sexual violence, ethnic violence, and crimes against the LGBT community. The success of this entire operation rested in part on the extent to which the SJP could import TJ capabilities from the academy, the judiciary, and civil society. So far, the SJP has recruited nearly 900 members of staff.[53] According to Botero (2017), the recruitment of 51 qualified judges was particularly crucial, and the challenge was met with success. The selection process was left to a committee of independent experts, who appointed justices with 'a variety of professional backgrounds, including but not limited to criminal law'. Crucially, these are not necessarily 'ones the FARC or the government would have picked'.

The SJP has between 15 and 20 years to complete its mission. Whether the weak political consensus around the peace can last that long is hard to tell. But so far, the SJP has moved at a reasonable pace, probably as a result of this ability to import and create TJ capabilities. In its first two years of existence, for example, the SJP opened 5 flagship cases involving 800,000 victims, and signed agreements with more than 9,000 ex-FARC members and 2,000 security agents so that their cases can be processed via this innovative TJ mechanism. The expectations that this initial momentum generates among victims and alleged perpetrators, coupled with the *espirit de corps* that is likely developing among SJP staff, might make it difficult for recalcitrant elites to dismantle the institution.

4 Why Latin America?

In this Element I discussed some of Latin America's key contributions to the history of TJ, focusing on innovations in trials and truth commissions since the 1980s. I also pointed out that while there is a general trend towards implementation of TJ policies, there is still important variation in achieved

---

[53] See www.jep.gov.co/Paginas/rendicion2019.aspx [accessed 6 June 2019].

'levels' of truth and justice. Scholars have developed two main theoretical frameworks to explain these temporal and cross-national differences: one that focuses on power politics, and another on international norms and social mobilization. I reviewed the merits and shortcomings of these schools of thought, and proposed a complementary framework that emphasizes the descriptive and explanatory importance of domestic processes of institutional change and capacity building. By way of conclusion, this final section discusses why Latin America became such an extraordinary site of innovation for TJ.

One important factor is that Latin America is home to Argentina, a global pioneer in the field. When Argentina transitioned to democracy in 1983, the notion of TJ did not exist. The policies introduced by the Alfonsín administration jump-started a long process of regional and international innovation that defined what we now think of as TJ. A combination of two conditions made the Argentine experience unique, and turned it into a highly visible and iconic moment in the history of TJ. This in turn inspired further experimentation across Latin America.

First, the crimes perpetrated by the military dictatorship were particularly pervasive and ruthless. More importantly, unlike victims of violence in the Peruvian or Central American conflicts, who were on average poor, indigenous, and rural, the Argentine military targeted urban middle-class victims, whose families had more social and economic capital to denounce the crimes at home and abroad. Some of these victims went into exile, and were able to use their middle-class professional skills in service of the cause. For example, Vecchioli (2010) shows how labour lawyers became human rights lawyers and started to weave international solidarity networks. Such resources and connections facilitated the early use of the Inter-American system and gave visibility to an otherwise peripheral state. The experiences accumulated during this time, especially in the legal field, thus laid the foundations for an unusually internationalized and highly professionalized human rights movement.

Second, the type of regime transition and the personal characteristics of the new president created an unparalleled window of opportunity for investigating and punishing past abuses at a time when this was not necessarily an imperative for countries emerging from violence. The rather unusual policies that were possible under these conditions attracted international attention almost immediately, becoming an object of study and admiration. Unlike most other transitional presidents, Alfonsín had access to minds of the calibre of Carlos Nino, who had the intellectual capacity to operationalize abstract human rights principles. The sophisticated justifications such thinkers provided for the administration's key innovations, as well as their ex-post reflections on the Argentine experiment, mapped the contours of future intellectual debates about TJ. It certainly helped that people such as Nino had international academic credentials, and were able to publish their work in prestigious English- and Spanish-language outlets.

This combination of conditions was not replicated in any other European or Latin American transition of the third wave. For instance, while the socio-demographic profile and international connections of Chilean victims were not entirely dissimilar, the type of transition meant the space for awe-inspiring innovations was more restricted. Similarly, while Greece implemented an innovative policy of criminal prosecutions before Argentina, the lack of an internationalized human rights movement meant that it never acquired the same visibility or iconic status (Sikkink 2011). By becoming an emblem of a new way of dealing with the past, Argentina thus shaped how other countries responded to similar dilemmas (Zunino 2019). Crucially, because ideas spread better within regions (Sikkink 2008), the impact of the Argentine case was especially strong in Latin America, igniting a uniquely productive struggle for truth and justice across the entire region.

What happened in Argentina in the 1980s had decisive positive and negative demonstration effects among its neighbours. On the one hand, it expanded the limits of what was imaginable and perceived as possible by victims and activists elsewhere. In this sense, the achievements of the Alfonsín government con-solidated the centrality of TJ in the political debates of Latin American transi-tioning societies. The Argentine experience was also a source of inspiration for practitioners. The trial against the juntas, for instance, was still an important reference point a quarter of a century later during the Fujimori trial (Gonzalez-Ocantos 2016a: 191–192). On the other hand, Alfonsín's policies, and the backlash that followed, forced elites in other countries facing much narrower windows of opportunity to find alternative ways to pursue TJ. This fuelled ingenuity and variation in TJ outcomes, especially in terms of truth-seeking efforts that could satisfy demands for accountability without risking democratic backsliding.

The timing of the Argentine experience also contributed to the early consolida-tion of a highly skilled cohort of TJ practitioners. Several graduates from this political experiment went on to occupy nodal points in the international human rights movement, and thus proved instrumental in the diffusion of experiences, practices, and ideas about TJ to countries grappling with similar questions. For example, Argentines were recruited to staff or advise truth commissions, helped create the International Center for Transitional Justice, and occupied important positions in human rights posts at the UN. Similarly, the Grandmothers of Plaza de Mayo, aided by international forensic experts and the EAAF, pioneered forensic exhumations and the use of genetic tests in the context of truth-seeking efforts in the 1980s. Since then, the EAAF has assisted victims and commissions around the region (and the globe) (Kovras 2017). As Kathryn Sikkink (2011: 94) puts it, 'each of these individuals ... acted as "human chains," linking together the Argentine experience with the rest of the world'.

As a region, Latin America displays strong tendencies towards the diffusion of ideas, policies, and institutions in a variety of areas, including democratization (Mainwaring and Pérez-Liñán 2013), economic reforms (Weyland 2006), and gender quota legislation (Krook 2009). In addition to the 'Argentina' effect, there are two more general conditions that turned TJ into yet another area where we see highly productive diffusion processes. First, despite important differences in the scope and patterns of violence, especially between countries that experienced dictatorship versus those that experienced armed conflicts, and in the politico-institutional settlements that put an end to violence and created more or less generous windows of opportunity for TJ, the wave of human rights abuses that affected Latin America between the 1960s and 1980s gave rise to constituencies with similar grievances. This fuelled a common desire for accountability that partly explains convergent regional patterns. More importantly, commonalities in the *types* of abuses inspired the promotion of innovative and comprehensive approaches to TJ throughout the region.

Latin American security forces perpetrated analogous crimes in different jurisdictions, most notably torture and forced disappearances. Such commonalities in repressive tactics were far from coincidental. In many ways, repression was a transnational affair. For example, military officers received similar training in counter-insurgency at the School of the Americas (Gill 2004). Some military regimes, in particular those of the Southern Cone, even coordinated repression across borders (Lessa 2015). The extremely high incidence of forced disappearances that resulted from these strategies played a crucial role in the future evolution of TJ policies, leading to the adoption of creative approaches. The crime of forced disappearance is a particularly perverse type of human rights violation because it radically negates both truth *and* justice and, as a result, deeply invests relatives and other groups in the fight for accountability. As Robben (2005: 284) puts it, the trauma inflicted by forced disappearances 'unleashes powerful political forces'. Specifically, the absence of information about the whereabouts of victims made it a categorial imperative to implement multidisciplinary truth-seeking efforts designed to speak for an otherwise silent state. As we saw in Section 1, the demand for closure that resulted from this state of affairs was so compelling that truth commissions succeeded even in transitional contexts where the political space for accountability was rather limited. The absence of information about the whereabouts of victims also complicated justice-seeking efforts. A more positive by-product, however, was the high degree of creativity on the part of those investigating and seeking punishment. Indeed, the need to overcome the legal and evidentiary challenges presented by forced disappearances was one of the key engines behind some of the most groundbreaking jurisprudential achievements of the IACtHR and several national courts.

This Element makes clear that innovations in international legal discourse played a fundamental role in cracking open these walls of silence and impunity, turning the field of TJ into a highly technical and legalized one (Zunino 2019). Although the culture of the legal academy and the bench across Latin America was until relatively recently quite hostile to international law – a phenomenon that explains why victims and their lawyers had to design creative strategies of judicial change – Latin American countries were not newcomers to the world of international legal innovations. Latin America's historic contributions to the field of international law are therefore the second, and final, background factor that likely facilitated diffusion and experimentation in the area of TJ.

Latin American elites developed rights-centred discourses long before independence (Carozza 2003), and according to Reus-Smit (2013:107), 'it was through the lens of rights' that they 'interpreted' distant developments in Europe, eventually triggering independence movements across the Spanish and Portuguese empires. Imbued in this tradition, members of the region's legal elite also became key players in the progress of international public law during the second half of the nineteenth century. Latin American thinkers made notable contributions to public debates about the principles of sovereignty and international peace, including, for example, Alberdi's *The Crime of War* (1870). As Scarfi (2017) shows, coupled with the development of international scholarly and diplomatic networks, such contributions consolidated the foundations of an Inter-American legal order in the first decades of the twentieth century. Despite the inherent tensions between the idea of international human rights and the emphasis on sovereignty and non-intervention characteristic of much of this foundational thinking, Latin Americans went on to thicken this nascent legal order with pioneering contributions to the global human rights regime.

In the immediate aftermath of World War II, Latin American delegations met in Colombia to draft the American Declaration of the Rights and Duties of Man, a move that allowed them to exert great influence during the UN's San Francisco conference responsible for the 1948 Universal Declaration of Human Rights (Glendon 2008; Sikkink 2017). Two decades later, the region consolidated this internationalist orientation by signing the American Convention on Human Rights (1969) and establishing the Inter-American human rights system, which was second only to the European one created in the 1950s (Goldman 2009). Initially stifled by Cold War politics and the spread of authoritarianism, the Inter-American human rights system became a focal point for continental legal innovation, networked activism, and international pressure, which, as we saw in Section 2, played a key role in the push for TJ. Finally, Latin America's contributions to the field of human rights law can be further seen in the development of a legal vocabulary to describe and punish mass atrocities. Lawyers based in the region were prominent members of a transnational network of criminal law experts who at different junctures throughout the twentieth century fought for the codification and criminalization of international crimes. This led to important breakthroughs in national penal legislation on mass atrocities as early as the 1970s. For example, in a fascinating account of the movement, Berlin (2015) shows how these experts brokered the inclusion of 'genocide' in the Guatemalan penal code of 1973.[54]

This brief overview shows that Latin American elites have long been plugged into a transnational space of legal innovation. The internationalist tradition spearheaded by prominent practitioners, as well as diplomatic and intellectual entrepreneurs, helped create a structural openness to a highly technical lexicon, set up critical institutional spaces, and nurtured civil society networks and expertise, all of which turned the region into fertile ground for TJ. Importantly, past developments somewhat naturalized the use of international legal discourses as tools of political struggle, improving the ability of pro-accountability actors in the 1990s and 2000s to engineer receptivity to unorthodox legal principles among institutional gate-keepers. Seen in this light, Latin America's groundbreaking contributions to TJ are less puzzling: they represent the continuation of a long tradition of intellectual and institutional advances in the area of fundamental rights and international public law.

---

[54] As a result of these early efforts to criminalize mass atrocity, the judges who convicted Ríos-Montt in 2013 did not have to rely on extemporaneous criminal definitions, but could use those that were part of the legal order at the time of perpetration.

References

Abrão, P. and M. Torelly. 2012. 'Resistance to Change: Brazil's Persistent Amnesty and its Alternatives for Truth and Justice'. In F. Lessa and L. Payne, eds, *Amnesty in the Age of Human Rights Accountability*. Cambridge: Cambridge University Press, pp. 152–181

Acuña, C. and C. Smulovitz. 1995. 'Militares en la transición argentina: del gobierno a la subordinación constitucional'. In C. Acuña et al. Juicio, castigo y memoria: derechos humanos y justicia en la política argentina. Buenos Aires: Nueva Visión, pp. 19–99

   1997. 'Guarding the Guardians in Argentina: Some Lessons about the Risks and Benefits of Empowering the Courts'. In J. McAdams, ed., *Transitional Justice and the Rule of Law in New Democracies*. Notre Dame: University of Notre Dame Press, pp. 93–111

Albarracín, J. and L. Gamboa. 2017. 'Public Opinion and Support for Transitional Justice in Colombia'. Paper presented at the annual meeting of the Southern Political Science Association, New Orleans, 26 December.

Ambos, K. 2011. 'The Fujimori Judgment: A President's Responsibility for Crimes Against Humanity as Indirect Perpetrator by Virtue of an Organized Power Apparatus'. *Journal of International Criminal Justice*, 9:137–158.

Anton, S. 2018. *The ICC's Inconsistent Approach to Complementary in Preliminary Examinations*. MPhil Thesis, University of Oxford.

Arthur, P. 2009. 'How Transitions Reshaped Human Rights: A Conceptual History of Transitional Justice'. *Human Rights Quarterly*, 31(2):321–367.

Arzobispado de Santiago. 1996. *Situación de los derechos humanos durante el primer semestre de 1996*. Available at: www.derechos.org/nizkor/chile/vicaria/informe1.html

Baird, E. and N. Roht-Arriaza. 2012. 'De Facto and De Jure Amnesty Laws: The Central American Case'. In F. Lessa and L. Payne, eds, *Amnesty in the Age of Human Rights Accountability*. Cambridge: Cambridge University Press, pp. 182–209

Balardini, L., A. Oberlin, and L. Sobredo. 2011. 'Violencia de género y abusos sexuales en los centros clandestinos de detención'. In *Hacer justicia: Nuevos debates sobre el juzgamiento de crímenes de lesa humanidad en Argentina*. Buenos Aires: Siglo XXI, pp. 167–225

Barnett, M. and M. Finnemore. 2004. *Rules for the World: International Organizations in Global Politics*. Ithaca: Cornell University Press.

Berlin, M. 2015. *The Criminalization of Atrocities in Domestic Legal Systems Since World War II.* Unpublished PhD Dissertation, University of California, Irvine.

Betancour, B., R. Figuereido, and T. Buergenthal. 1993. *From Madness to Hope: The 12-year War in El Salvador.* Washington: USIP.

Brett, R. 2016. 'Peace Without Reconciliation? Understanding the Trial against Generals Ríos-Montt and Rodríguez-Salazar in the Wake of Guatemala's Genocide'. *Journal of Genocide Research*, 18(2):285–303.

Botero, S. 2017. 'Colombia's Special Criminal Tribunal: Justicia Especial para la Paz'. *International Journal of Constitutional Law Blog*, 15 October.

Burt, J. M. 2009. 'Guilty as Charged: The Trial of Former Peruvian President Alberto Fujimori for Human Rights Violations'. *The International Journal of Transitional Justice*, 3(3):384–405.

  2016. 'From Heaven to Hell in Ten Days: The Genocide Trial in Guatemala'. *Journal of Genocide Research*, 18(2):143–169.

Burt, J. M., G. Fried, and F. Lessa. 2013. 'Civil Society and the Resurgent Struggle against Impunity in Uruguay (1986–2012)'. *International Journal of Transitional Justice*, 7(2):306–327.

Carozza, P. (2003) 'From Conquest to Constitutions: Retrieving a Latin American Tradition of the Idea of Human Rights'. *Human Rights Quarterly*, 25(2):281–313.

Cassel, D. 1996. 'Lessons from the Americas: Guidelines for International Response to Amnesties for Atrocities'. *Law and Contemporary Problems*, 59(4):197–224.

CIDE. 2018. *Estudio para elaborar una propusta de política pública en materia de Justicia Transicional en México.* Mexico City: CIDE.

Collins, C. 2011. *Post-Transitional Justice: Human Rights Trials in Chile and El Salvador.* University Park: Pennsylvania State University Press.

  2018. 'Verdad, justicia y memoria en Chile a dos décadas del Caso Pinochet'. In *Informe anual sobre derechos humanos en Chile 2018*. Santiago: Universidad Diego Portales, pp. 17–105

Collins, C. and B. Hau. 2016. 'Chile: Incremental Truth, Late Justice'. In E. Skaar, J. García-Godos, and C. Collins, eds., *Transitional Justice in Latin America*. London: Routledge, pp. 126–150

Comisión de la Verdad y Reconciliación. 2003. *Informe Final.* Lima: CVR.

CONADEP. 1984. *Nunca Más.* Buenos Aires: EUDEBA.

Crenzel, E. 'Argentina's National Commission on the Disappearance of Persons: Contributions to Transitional Justice'. *The International Journal of Transitional Justice*, 2:173–191.

de Grieff, P., ed. 2008. *The Handbook of Reparations*. Oxford: Oxford University Press.

Eliaschev, P. 2011. *Los hombres del juicio*. Buenos Aires: Sudamericana.

Elster, J. 2004. *Closing the Books*. Cambridge: Cambridge University Press.

Engstrom, P., ed. 2019. *The Inter-American Human Rights System: Impact Beyond Compliance*. London: Palgrave.

Ensalaco, M. 1994. 'Truth Commissions for Chile and El Salvador'. *Human Rights Quarterly*, 16(4):656–675.

Evans, R. 2007. 'Treating Poorly Healed Wounds: Partisan Choices and Human Rights Policies in Latin America'. *Human Rights Review*, 8(3):249–276.

Gill, L. 2004. *The School of the Americas*. Durham: Duke University Press.

Glendon, M. 2008. 'The Forgotten Crucible: The Latin American Influence on the Universal Human Rights Idea'. *Harvard Human Rights Journal*, 16:27–39.

Goldman, R. 2009. 'History and Action: The Inter-American Human Rights System and the Role of the Inter-American Commission of Human Rights'. *Human Rights Quarterly*, 31(4):856–887.

Gonzalez-Cueva, E. 2004. 'The Contributions of the Peruvian Truth and Reconciliation Commission to Prosecutions'. *Criminal Law Forum*, 15 (1–2):55–66.

Gonzalez-Ocantos, E. 2014. 'Persuade Them or Oust Them: Crafting Judicial Change and Transitional Justice in Argentina'. *Comparative Politics*, 46 (4):479–498.

    2016a. *Shifting Legal Visions: Judicial Change and Human Rights Trials in Latin America*. Cambridge: Cambridge University Press.

    2016b. 'Evaluations of Human Rights Trials and Trust in Judicial Institutions: Evidence from Fujimori's Trial in Peru'. *The International Journal of Human Rights*, 20(4):445–470.

    2018. 'Communicative Entrepreneurs: The Inter-American Court of Human Rights' Dialogue with National Judges'. *International Studies Quarterly*, 62(4):737–750.

Hayner, P. 2010. *Unspeakable Truths: Transitional Justice and the Challenge of Truth Commissions*. London: Routledge.

Hilbink, L. 2007. *Judges Beyond Politics in Democracy and Dictatorship: Lessons from Chile*. Cambridge: Cambridge University Press.

Hillebrecht, C., A. Huneeus and S. Borda. 2018. 'The Judicialization of Peace'. *Harvard International Law Journal*, 59(2):279–330.

Huneeus, A. 2010. 'Judging from a Guilty Conscience: The Chilean Judiciary's Human Rights Turn'. *Law & Social Inquiry*, 35(1):99–135.

Huntington, S. 1991. *The Third Wave: Democratization in the Late Twentieth Century*. London: University of Oklahoma Press.

International Crisis Group. 2011. *Learning to Walk Without a Crutch: An Assessment of the International Commission Against Impunity in Guatemala*. ICG Latin America Report N. 36.

Karl, T. 2007. 'The Justice Cascade in Latin America'. *Santa Clara Journal of International Law*, 5(2):345–362.

Keck, M. and K. Sikkink. 1998. *Activists Beyond Borders: Advocacy Networks in International Politics*. Ithaca: Cornell University Press.

Kemp, S. 2014. 'Guatemala Prosecutes Former President Ríos-Montt'. *Journal of International Criminal Justice*, 12(1):133–156.

Kirtz, N. ed. 1995. *Transitional Justice*. Washington: USIP.

Krook, M. L. 2009. *Quotas for Women in Politics: Gender and Candidate Selection Reform Worldwide*. Oxford: Oxford University Press.

Kovras, I. 2017. *Grassroots Activism and the Evolution of Transitional Justice*. Cambridge: Cambridge University Press.

LaPlante, L. and K. Theidon. 2006. 'Transitional Justice in Times of Conflict: Colombia's Ley de Justicia y Paz'. *Michigan Journal of International Law*, 49(1):49–106.

Lessa, F. 2012. 'Barriers to Justice: The *Ley de Caducidad* and Impunity in Uruguay'. In F. Lessa and L. Payne, eds, *Amnesty in the Age of Human Rights Accountability*. Cambridge: Cambridge University Press, pp. 123–151

   2015. 'Justice Beyond Borders: The Operation Condor Trial and Accountability for Transnational Crimes in South America'. *International Journal of Transitional Justice*, 9(3):494–506.

   2019. *Investigating Crimes Against Humanity in South America*. Policy Brief, University of Oxford.

Lessa, F. and L. Payne, eds. 2012. *Amnesty in the Age of Human Rights Accountability*. Cambridge: Cambridge University Press.

Lessa, F., T. Olsen, L. Payne, G. Pereira, and A. Reiter. 2014. 'Overcoming Impunity: Pathways to Accountability in Latin America'. *International Journal of Transitional Justice*, 8(1):75–98

Lutz, E. and K. Sikkink. 2000. 'International Human Rights Law and Practice in Latin America'. *International Organization*, 54(3):633–659.

   2001. 'The Justice Cascade: Evolution and Impact of Foreign Human Rights Trials in Latin America'. *Chicago Journal of International Law*, 2(1):1–33.

Mainwaring, S. and A. Pérez-Liñán. 2013. *Democracies and Dictatorships in Latin America*. Cambridge: Cambridge University Press.

Mallinder, L. 2008. 'Exploring the Practice of States in Introducing Amnesties'. In K. Ambos, J. Large, and M. Wierda, eds, *Building a Future on Peace and Justice*. Berlin: Springer, pp. 127–171

Martínez-Barahona, E. and M. Gutiérrez-Salazar. 2016. 'El Salvador: The Difficult Fight Against Impunity'. In E. Skaar, J. García-Godos, and C. Collins, eds, *Transitional Justice in Latin America*. London: Routledge, pp. 178–202

Mayer-Rieckh, A. and P. de Grieff. 2008. *Justice as Prevention: Vetting Public Employees in Transitional Societies*. New York: Social Science Research Council.

Méndez, J. 1997. 'In Defence of Transitional Justice'. In J. McAdams, ed., *Transitional Justice and the Rule of Law in New Democracies*. Notre Dame: University of Notre Dame Press, pp. 1–26

 2010. 'Significance of the Fujimori Trial'. *American University International Law Review*, 25(4):649–656.

Michel, V. 2018. *Prosecutorial Accountability and Victims' Rights in Latin America*. Cambridge: Cambridge University Press.

Michel, V. and K. Sikkink. 2013. 'Human Rights Prosecutions and the Participation Rights of Victims in Latin America'. *Law & Society Review*, 47(4):873–907.

Nino, C. 1991. 'The Duty to Punish Past Abuses of Human Rights Put into Context: The Case of Argentina'. *Yale Law Journal*, 100(8):2619–2640.

 1996. *Radical Evil on Trial*. New Haven: Yale University Press.

Norden. D. 1996. *Military Rebellion in Argentina*. Lincoln: University of Nebraska Press.

O'Donnell, G. and P. Schmitter. 1986. *Transitions from Authoritarian Rule: Tentative Conclusions about Uncertain Democracies*. Baltimore: The John Hopkins University Press.

Olsen, T., L. Payne, and A. Reiter. 2010. *Transitional Justice in Balance*. Washington: USIP.

Open Society. 2015. *Unfinished Business: Guatemala's International Commission Against Impunity (CICIG)*. March Briefing, OSJI.

Orentlicher, D. 1991. 'Settling Accounts: The Duty to Prosecute Human Rights Violations of a Prior Regime'. *Yale Law Journal*, 100(8):2537–2615.

Osiel, M. 1986. 'The Making of Human Rights Policy in Argentina: The Impact of Ideas and Interests on Legal Conflict'. *Yale Law Journal*, 100:2537–2618.

Payne, L. 2008. *Unsettling Accounts: Neither Truth nor Reconciliation in Confessions of State Violence*. Durham: Duke University Press.

Pion-Berlin, D. 1994. 'To Prosecute or to Pardon? Human Rights Decisions in the Latin American Southern Cone'. *Human Rights Quarterly*, 16 (1):105–130.

Procuraduría de Crímenes Contra la Humanidad. 2018. *Informe estadístico sobre el estado de las causas por delitos de lesa humanidad en Argentina*. Buenos Aires: MPF.

Prusak, C. 2010. 'The Trial of Alberto Fujimori: Navigating the Show Trial Dilemma in Pursuit of Transitional Justice'. *NYU Law Review*, 85 (3):867–904.

Reus-Smit, C. 2013. *Individual Rights and the Making of the International System*. Cambridge: Cambridge University Press.

Risse-Kappen, T. and K. Sikkink. 1999. 'The Socialization of International Human Rights Norms into Domestic Practices: Introduction'. In T. Risse-Kappen, S. Ropp, and K. Sikkink, eds, *The Power of Human Rights*. Cambridge: Cambridge University Press, pp. 1–38

Robben, A. 2005. *Political Violence and Trauma in Argentina*. Philadelphia: University of Pennsylvania Press.

Roehrig, T. 2009. 'Executive Leadership and the Continuing Quest for Justice in Argentina'. *Human Rights Quarterly*, 31(3):721–747.

Roht-Arriaza, N. 1995. 'Conclusion'. In N. Roht-Arriaza, ed., *Impunity and Human Rights in International Law and Practice*. Cambridge: Cambridge University Press, pp. 181–304

  2006. *The Pinochet Effect*. Philadelphia: University of Pennsylvania Press.

  2015. 'After Amnesties are Gone: Latin American National Courts and the New Contours of the Fight Against Impunity'. *Human Rights Quarterly* 37 (2):341–382.

Roht-Arriaza, N. and L. Gibson. 1998. 'The Developing Jurisprudence on Amnesty'. *Human Rights Quarterly*, 20:843–885.

Rowen, J. 2018. *Searching for Truth in the Transitional Justice Movement*. Cambridge: Cambridge University Press.

Scarfi, J. P. 2017. *The Hidden History of International Law in the Americas*. Oxford: Oxford University Press.

Scott, J. 1998. *Seeing Like a State*. New Haven: Yale University Press.

Seils, P. 2004. 'Promised Unfulfilled? The Special Prosecutor's Office in Mexico'. Occasional Paper Series, ICTJ.

Sharp, D. 2012. 'Addressing Economic Violence in Times of Transition: Towards Positive-Pace Paradigm for Transitional Justice'. *Fordham International Law Journal*, 35(3):780–813.

Sikkink, K. 1993. 'Human Rights, Principled-Issue Networks, and Sovereignty in Latin America'. *International Organization*, 47(3):411–441.

  2005. 'The Transnational Dimension of the Judicialization of Politics in Latin America'. In R. Sieder, L. Schjolden and A. Angell, eds, *The Judicialization of Politics in Latin America*. London: Palgrave, pp. 263–292

2008. 'From Pariah State to Global Protagonist: Argentina and the Struggle for International Human Rights'. *Latin American Politics and Society*, 50 (1):1–29.

2011. *The Justice Cascade*. New York: Norman.

2017. *Evidence for Hope*. Princeton: Princeton University Press.

Skaar, E. 2011. *Judicial Independence and Human Rights in Latin America*. London: Palgrave.

Speck, P. 1987. 'The Trial of the Argentine Junta: Responsibilities and Realities'. *University of Miami Inter-American Law Review*, 18(3):491–531.

Supreme Court of Justice of Peru. 2010. 'The Judgement against Fujimori for Human Rights Violations [Aimee Sullivan, trans.]'. *American University International Law Review*, 25:657–838.

Teitel, R. 2000. *Transitional Justice*. Oxford: Oxford University Press.

2003. 'Transitional Justice Genealogy'. *Harvard Human Rights Journal*, 16:69–94.

United Nations. 2004. 'Report of the Secretary-General on the Rule of Law and Transitional Justice in Conflict and Post-Conflict Societies'. UN-Doc S/2004/616.

2010. 'United Nations Approach to Transitional Justice'. Guidance Notes of the Secretary-General.

2015. 'Report of the Special Rapporteur on the promotion of truth, justice, reparation and guarantees of non-recurrence'. UN-Doc A/HRC/30/42.

2017. 'Report of the Special Rapporteur on the Promotion of Truth, Justice, Reparation, and Guarantees of Non-recurrence'. UN-Doc A/HRC/36/50.

Vecchioli, V. 2010. 'Derechos humanos y compromiso militante'. Unpublished manuscript.

Weyland, K. 2006. *Bounded Rationality and Policy Diffusion: Social Sector Reform in Latin America*. Princeton: Princeton University Press.

Yankelevich, J. 2018. *El canto del cisne de la FEMOSPP: la única condena a un perpetrador de la guerra sucia en Mexico*. Unpublished Manuscript.

Yashar, D. 2018. *Homicidal Ecologies: Illicit Economies and Complicit States in Latin America*. Cambridge: Cambridge University Press.

Zalaquett, J. 1990. 'Confronting Human Rights Violations Perpetrated by Former Governments: Applicable Principles and Political Constraints'. *Hamline Law Review*, 13:623–660.

1995. 'Confronting Human Rights Violations Committed by Former Governments: Principles Applicable and Political Constraints'. In N. Kirtz, ed., *Transitional Justice*. Washington: USIP, pp. 3–31

Zunino, M. 2019. *Justice Framed: A Genealogy of Transitional Justice*. Cambridge: Cambridge University Press.

Cambridge Elements ⹀

Elements in Politics and Society in Latin America

Maria Victoria Murillo
Columbia University

Maria Victoria Murillo is Professor of Political Science and International Affairs at Columbia University. She is the author of *Political Competition, Partisanship, and Policymaking in the Reform of Latin American Public Utilities* (Cambridge, 2009). She is also editor of *Carreras Magisteriales, Desempeño Educativo y Sindicatos de Maestros en América Latina* (2003), and co-editor of *Argentine Democracy: The Politics of Institutional Weakness* (2005). She has published in edited volumes as well as in the *American Journal of Political Science, World Politics, Comparative Political Studies* among others.

Juan Pablo Luna
The Pontifical Catholic University of Chile

Juan Pablo Luna is Professor in the Department of Political Science at The Pontifical Catholic University of Chile. He is the author of *Segmented Representation. Political Party Strategies in Unequal Democracies*, and has co-authored *Latin American Party Systems* (Cambridge, 2010). His work on political representation, state capacity, and organized crime has appeared in *Comparative Political Studies, Revista de Ciencia Política*, the *Journal of Latin American Studies, Latin American Politics and Society, Studies in Comparative International Development* among others.

Tulia G. Falleti
University of Pennsylvania

Tulia G. Falleti is the Class of 1965 Term Associate Professor of Political Science, Director of the Latin American and Latino Studies Program, and Senior Fellow of the Leonard Davis Institute for Health Economics at the University of Pennsylvania. She is the author of the award-winning *Decentralization and Subnational Politics in Latin America* (Cambridge, 2010). She is co-editor of *The Oxford Handbook of Historical Institutionalism*, among other edited books. Her articles have appeared in many edited volumes and journals, such as the *American Political Science Review* and *Comparative Political Studies*.

Andrew Schrank
Brown University

Andrew Schrank is the Olive C. Watson Professor of Sociology and International & Public Affairs at Brown University. His articles on business, labor, and the state in Latin America have appeared in the *American Journal of Sociology, Comparative Politics, Comparative Political Studies, Latin American Politics & Society, Social Forces*, and *World Development*, among other journals, and his co-authored book, *Root-Cause Regulation: Labor Inspection in Europe and the Americas*, is out soon.

About the Series
Latin American politics and society are at a crossroads, simultaneously confronting serious challenges and remarkable opportunities that are likely to be shaped by formal institutions and informal practices alike. The new Politics and Society in Latin America Cambridge Elements series will offer multidisciplinary and methodologically pluralist contributions on the most important topics and problems confronted by the region.

Elements in Politics and Society in Latin America

Elements in the Series

*Understanding Institutional Weakness: Power and Design
in Latin American Institutions*
Daniel M. Brinks, Steven Levitsky and Maria Victoria Murillo